Colorlines | Brittany Shoot

". . . the newly released *Narrative of the Life of Frederick Douglass, An American Slave, Written by Himself: A New Critical Edition* brings together two of the great philosophical writers and racial justice activists of the last two centuries and combines the deeply personal writings of Frederick Douglass with several politically charged lectures given by Angela Y. Davis in the early 1970s. . . . Even for those who have never studied either writer in depth, Davis explores the many ways we can interpret Douglass's anti-slavery writing today and draws parallels between the continued oppression of women and prisoners. . . . The breadth of Davis's work in the past two decades is an inspiring example of bridge-building across causes and generations. That her contemporary activism can be coupled so flawlessly with Douglass's historic writings and powerful legacy speaks to the importance of their combined influence spanning centuries. . . . At a time when the freedoms once granted by the Fourteenth Amendment are now being applied to corporate entities, cannabilizing the legacy of freed slaves in the United States, this book—Davis's call for a more engaged electorate—is wonderfully timely and deeply engaging."

Huffington Post | Rick Ayres

"Douglass's description of his life in slavery, his resistance, and his flight to freedom could not be more timely or more meaningful to students. At a time when education officials are wringing their hands about how difficult it is to teach black students literacy, Douglass demonstrates how the struggle for literacy has always been a part of the struggle for liberation. . . . This is where Angela Davis injects her considerable insight. Her introduction connects Douglass's critique to the struggles for liberation in the 1960s and '70s, demonstrating the same courage, audacity, and clarity of vision that was required to see through and defy the slave system."

Regal Magazine | Judith Brown
"In her most diplomatic method, Davis proves what I never realized until now: The Black American slave era was not so much about Blacks and slavery as it was about the state of all humanity. . . . Davis shows in this very compelling volume that Frederick Douglass was simply a man. And what all men and women were meant to be . . . free."

The Midwest Book Review
"Being an educated man of color was a true anomaly in [Douglass's] day. *Narrative of the Life of Frederick Douglass: An American Slave* discusses Douglass's famous autobiography as Angela Y. Davis offers much studious insight. She examines Douglass's writings and how the man embraced intellectualism and spirituality to pull himself out of his subservient life in a society that thought of him as an animal. *Narrative of the Life of Frederick Douglass* is a must for anyone trying to get a greater understanding of the black icon."

Drums In The Global Village | Todd Steven Burroughs
"[Davis] uses Douglass to examine the philosophy of freedom. . . . [She] dissects Douglass's strengths and pitfalls of how he defined freedom—a definition that, Davis explains, leaves enslaved women behind as symbols of oppression, unable to achieve the "manhood" Douglass equates with his liberation. . . . The two pioneering feminists merge together, in theory and in practice, on the nature(s) of liberation. In this book of merged centuries, freedom travels from idea to action (creating resistance) to finally, negotiating a complex reality. Davis, in 2009 : "Many of us thought [in the 1960s and 1970s] that liberation was simply a question of organizing to *leverage power* from the hands of those we deemed to be the oppressors." An idea whose time has gone in the Obama era, one in which, supposedly, the ultimate power has been leveraged, but from whom and for what? This new version of an old book is a perfect excuse to analyze (Douglass's and Davis's) views of freedom as we continue to debate the Black movement's purpose in the second decade of the new century."

NARRATIVE OF THE LIFE OF FREDERICK DOUGLASS, AN AMERICAN SLAVE,

WRITTEN BY HIMSELF

A New Critical Edition
by Angela Y. Davis
including her
"Lectures on Liberation"

NARRATIVE OF THE LIFE OF
FREDERICK DOUGLASS,
AN AMERICAN SLAVE,

WRITTEN BY HIMSELF

A New Critical Edition
by Angela Y. Davis
including her
"Lectures on Liberation"

Open Media Series | City Lights Books
San Francisco

The Open Media Series is edited by Greg Ruggiero and archived by the Tamiment Library at New York University.

Cover design by John Yates at Stealworks.
Interior design by Linda Ronan.

Library of Congress Cataloging-in-Publication Data
Douglass, Frederick, 1818–1895.
 Narrative of the life of Frederick Douglass, an American slave, written by himself : a new critical edition / by Angela Y. Davis.
  p. cm. — (Open media series)
 Includes bibliographical references.
 ISBN 978-0-87286-527-3
 1. Douglass, Frederick, 1818–1895. 2. African American abolitionists—Biography. 3. Abolitionists—United States—Biography. 4. Slaves—United States—Biography. 5. Slavery—United States—History. I. Davis, Angela Y. (Angela Yvonne), 1944– II. Title.

E449.D749 2009b
973.8092—dc22
[B]
            2009032955

City Lights Books are published at the City Lights Bookstore, 261 Columbus Avenue, San Francisco, CA 94133.
www.citylights.com

CONTENTS

The idea for this book came in 2008. It was an election year, and millions of people were organizing to elect Barack Hussein Obama forty-fourth president of the United States. During the months of intense campaigning, the issue of race entered the national conversation and simmered in the background until the controversy surrounding the Obama family's minister, Reverend Jeremiah Wright, brought the issue to a full boil. Obama's response to the controversy came in Philadelphia on March 18, 2008. In a speech that included references to America's "original sin of slavery" and the history of the struggle for equal rights, Obama said, "Words on a parchment would not be enough to deliver slaves from bondage, or provide men and women of every color and creed their full rights and obligations as citizens of the United States. What would be needed were Americans in successive generations who were willing to do their part—through protests and struggle, on the streets and in the courts, through a civil war and civil disobedience and always at great risk—to narrow that gap between the promise of our ideals and the reality of their time."[1] The country, at least for a moment, was talking about its history and the roles slavery, race, and social struggle have played in making us who we are.

One of several books I was working on at the time was *The Meaning of Freedom*, a selection of transcripts of public talks by Angela Y. Davis (City Lights, 2010). In my research, I came across a reference to a small pamphlet titled *Lectures on Liberation*. Published by the NY Committee to Free Angela Davis sometime during her year-and-half incarceration, the pamphlet was originally sold for fifty cents a copy to raise funds for her legal defense. I purchased it online for forty dollars. When the slim, red staple-bound pamphlet arrived, I cut through the packaging carefully and felt like I was opening a time capsule. I sat down to read the two powerful lectures about Frederick Douglass, race, and resistance, and I was riveted. As a reader I was discovering a historic and invaluable out-of-print movement pamphlet, and as an editor I became excited by the possibility of sharing it with a new generation of readers, young people and educators. What better political moment could there be to publish these texts and introduce Angela Davis and Frederick Douglass together—two of the most important abolitionist intellectuals in U.S. history? I called Angela to share my excitement at having read the pamphlet, and during conversation the idea for this book was born.

The original *Lectures on Liberation* pamphlet contains three texts—transcripts of two lectures on Frederick Douglass, philosophy, and freedom that Davis delivered in

LECTURES ON LIBERATION

ANGELA Y. DAVIS

50¢

the fall of 1969 at UCLA, a year before her arrest, and a letter of support written and signed by over two dozen of her fellow faculty at UCLA during the period of her incarceration and legal defense. Her colleagues' inspired introduction describes the political context in which the lectures were delivered and their broader significance: "It was, we thought, a vindication of academic freedom and democratic education. For the lectures are a part of an attempt to bring to light the forbidden history of the enslavement and oppression of black people, and to place that history in an illuminating philosophical context. At the same time, they are sensitive, original and incisive; the work of an excellent teacher and a truly fine scholar."

Angela Davis was a young, multilingual scholar who had graduated *magna cum laude* from Brandeis University, and while studying under Herbert Marcuse to earn her doctorate she had accepted a two-year teaching appointment in the philosophy department at the University of California in Los Angeles. On July 1, 1969, William T. Divale, an undercover agent of the F.B.I., published a statement in the *Daily Bruin* that the UCLA philosophy department has just hired an assistant professor who was a Communist, and on July 9, 1969 the *San Francisco Examiner* identified the professor to be Angela Y. Davis. Richard Nixon was president, Ronald Reagan was governor of California, and when the news reached the university's board of regents, they fired Davis before the semester had begun. Her termination sparked considerable controversy, protest, and national media coverage.[2] With a groundswell of grassroots support, Davis fought back. In an act of resistance, she showed up for the first day of her course, "Recurring Philosophical Themes in Black Literature."[3] Expecting to deliver a lecture to the 166 students who had enrolled in the class, she instead found more than 1,500 members of the UCLA student body and faculty assembled in a show of support. The lecture she delivered that day is one of two talks about Frederick Douglass in the pamphlet and is presented here in book form for the first time.

As soon as the idea for this book was born, one of the first people with whom I discussed it was Mumia Abu-Jamal. At the time I was working with him on his book *Jailhouse Lawyers: Prisoners Defending Prisoners vs. The USA* (City Lights, 2009), for which Davis had written an introduction. Mumia would call me collect from Death Row, and we'd just as often spend most our fifteen-minute conversations discussing politics, race, and Obama as we would talk about the book.[4] Could Obama win? What would it mean for liberation struggle?

In a written interview I conducted with Mumia that was posted on *Z-net* after the election, he wrote:

> Social movements open up the eyes of the people, and present them with new ways of looking at the world, and hopefully moving in the world. Think about this. Everybody (esp. in the so-called left) is hyped about Obama's

election. As I wrote in a commentary last year, Mexico had a Black president over a century ago. If the abolition movement didn't fold their tents after the Civil War, and instead fought for broader, deeper social change, why couldn't Frederick Douglass have been elected president in 1870? To be sure, he was among the most brilliant men in the country; with eloquence, and erudition far beyond most men. He was financially and socially stable, and was one of the most respected men in the English world. As an ex-slave, his election would've set the lock and death-knell to slavery (instead of the hidden legalization of it thru the prison-industrial-complex), and made the Reconstruction Amendments real. Social movements have to have the ability to see beyond today's horizon, and have to have the stamina to work for social change. With social movements, everything is possible; without them, nothing is possible.[5]

Angela Davis, like Mumia Abu-Jamal, is more concerned with the people whose work drives social movements than the elected leaders and the legal system. In a public talk she delivered in Denver on February 15, 2008, she said:

I'm always very cautious when it comes to electoral politics. I think that particularly here in this country we have a tendency to invest our own collective power in individuals. We have what I sometimes call a messiah complex. This is why, when we think of the Civil Rights movement, we think of Martin Luther King. We can't imagine that that movement could have been created by huge numbers of people whose names we do not even know. We can't imagine that.

I often emphasize that the Montgomery bus boycott, which for many people is a defining moment of the Civil Rights movement, would not have been possible had it not been for black women domestic workers. These are the people we never think about. They are totally invisible, invisible in history, but those are the women who refused to ride the bus. Those are the black people who were riding the bus because they were riding from black communities to white communities because they were cleaning up white people's houses and cooking white people's food and doing their laundry. But we can't imagine that they were the agents of history that gave us this amazing civil rights movement.

All of which is to say this enthusiasm, this incredible enthusiasm that's been generated over the last period that has been called a movement, and Obama has specifically referred to what's happening around his campaign as a movement. If it is to be a movement, it has to demand much more than the election of a single individual, no matter what that individual may represent.[6]

It is in that spirit that this book is published—to increase our political literacy as a step toward demanding more of our current political moment. I use the word *literacy* intentionally because of the primary role that learning to read played in Frederick Douglass's learning to resist. In his passage on the subject in *Narrative* we see that it is through the defiant act of teaching himself to read that Douglass underwent an inner shift that empowered him to think independently of—and ultimately break free from—his white enslavers:

> Very soon after I went to live with Mr. and Mrs. Auld, she very kindly commenced to teach me the A, B, C. After I had learned this, she assisted me in learning to spell words of three or four letters. Just at this point of my progress, Mr. Auld found out what was going on, and at once forbade Mrs. Auld to instruct me further, telling her, among other things, that it was unlawful, as well as unsafe, to teach a slave to read. To use his own words, further, he said, "If you give a nigger an inch, he will take an ell. A nigger should know nothing but to obey his master—to do as he is told to do. Learning would spoil the best nigger in the world. Now," said he, "if you teach that nigger (speaking of myself) how to read, there would be no keeping him. It would forever unfit him to be a slave. He would at once become unmanageable, and of no value to his master. As to himself, it could do him no good, but a great deal of harm. It would make him discontented and unhappy." These words sank deep into my heart, stirred up sentiments within that lay slumbering, and called into existence an entirely new train of thought. It was a new and special revelation, explaining dark and mysterious things, with which my youthful understanding had struggled, but struggled in vain. I now understood what had been to me a most perplexing difficulty—to wit, the white man's power to enslave the black man. It was a grand achievement, and

I prized it highly. From that moment, I understood the
pathway from slavery to freedom.

Throughout her more than forty years as a movement
worker, author and educator, Angela Davis has worked cease-
lessly to further understand and clear the pathways from
slavery to freedom. She has written about Douglass both as
a way of better understanding the impact and limitations of
his work and as a way of analyzing how institutional racism
enforced by legal slavery continued after the passage of the
Thirteenth, Fourteenth and Fifteenth Amendments.

In her pioneering and critically acclaimed study published
in 1981, *Women, Race & Class,* Davis discusses the historic
role Douglass played in the nineteenth-century movement
for women's liberation and his achievement of "officially
introducing the issue of women's rights to the Black Liberation movement, where it was enthusiastically welcomed."
"Frederick Douglass," she writes, "the country's leading
Black abolitionist, was also the most prominent male advocate of women's emancipation in his time."[7] She describes
the impact he had at the first women's rights convention,
the Seneca Falls Convention of 1848:

> Among the approximately three hundred women and
> men attending the Seneca Falls Convention, the is-
> sue of electoral power for women was the only major
> point of contention: the suffrage resolution alone was

not unanimously endorsed. That the controversial proposal was presented at all, however, was due to Frederick
Douglass's willingness to second [Elizabeth Cady]
Stanton's motion and to employ his oratorical abilities
in defense of women's right to vote.

During those early days when women's rights was not
yet a legitimate cause, when woman suffrage was unfa-
miliar and unpopular as a demand, Frederick Douglass
publicly agitated for the political equality of women. In
the immediate aftermath of the Seneca Falls Convention, he published an editorial in his newspaper, the
North Star. Entitled "The Rights of Women," its content
was quite radical for the times: "In respect to political
rights, we hold woman to be justly entitled to all we
claim for men. We go farther, and express our conviction that all political rights which it is expedient for man
to exercise, it is equally so for woman. All that distin-
guishes man as an intelligent and accountable being, is
equally true of woman."[8]

In her studies of the prison-industrial-complex and her
advocacy for the abolition of prisons, Davis closely analyz-
es the unbroken continuum between the slavery Douglass
experienced in the nineteenth century, the racist terror-
ism she survived growing up in segregated Alabama,[9] and
today's interconnected problems of economic and political subjugation, prisons, capital punishment, police brutality, and the women, immigrants, and communities of
color most impacted by them. One hundred fifty years after

Frederick Douglass fearlessly organized social movements and personally lobbied a reluctant President Abraham Lincoln to abolish slavery,[10] Angela Y. Davis continues the tradition and describes her work today as "forging a twenty-first-century abolitionist movement." In constructing her model of abolitionism, Davis draws deeply from W. E. B. DuBois and his concept of "abolition democracy"—the idea that U.S. democracy is inauthentic and compromised, and will continue to be until all institutions that perpetrate injustice and domination are replaced because "democracy for blacks had been withheld at the very moment it had been promised: upon the abolition of slavery."[11] In her book with Eduardo Mendieta, *Abolition Democracy*, she writes:

> DuBois pointed out that in order to fully abolish the oppressive conditions produced by slavery, new democratic institutions would have to be created. Because this did not occur, black people encountered new forms of slavery—from debt peonage and the convict lease system[12] to segregated and second-class education. The prison system continues to carry out this terrible legacy. It has become a receptacle for all of those human beings who bear the inheritance of the failure to create abolition democracy in the aftermath of slavery. And this inheritance is not only borne by black prisoners, but by poor Latino, Native American, Asian, and white prisoners. Moreover, its use as such a receptacle for people who are deemed the detritus of society is on the rise throughout the world.[13]

Angela Davis continues to write, to agitate, to educate and to speak out in solidarity with global movements against racism, sexism, and political repression. As forms of oppression dating back to slavery still manifest today, so too do networks of resistance, creativity and hope. She urges us to join them. She urges us, with Douglass as a metaphor, to continue the work of the oppressed women and men whose struggles precede us. She urges us to increase our own levels of political literacy and critical engagement as defiant steps toward demanding—and winning—greater justice and freedom that we can all experience and enjoy together.

—Greg Ruggiero
October 2009
Brooklyn

INTRODUCTION TO THE CITY LIGHTS EDITION OF
Narrative of the Life of Frederic Douglass, An American Slave

It has been more than a century and a half since *Narrative of the Life of Frederick Douglass, An American Slave* was first published. The text garnered a broad readership among Douglass's abolitionist contemporaries in the United States and Britain and later came to be regarded as the paradigmatic American Slave Narrative.

It is well known that Frederick Douglass wrote his first autobiography in 1845 in part to dispel doubts about his status as a fugitive slave. In the abolitionist circuit, white audiences were often so impressed by his literacy and eloquence as a speaker that they assumed he must have been a free black person who was formally educated. According to an article in the *Liberator*, the most important abolitionist journal of that period,

> Many persons in the audience seemed unable to credit the statements which he gave of himself, and could not believe that he was actually a slave. How a man, only six years out of bondage, and who had never gone to school a day in his life, could speak with such eloquence—with

such precision of language and power of thought—they
were utterly at a loss to devise.[14]

Some scholars have also argued that William Lloyd Garrison and other abolitionist leaders expected Douglass to confine his remarks to his own experience as a slave, leaving the analytical dimension to white speakers. By writing his autobiography, Douglass felt that he would not only be able to present irrefutable evidence of his background, but he would also be able to focus more freely on analyses of slavery and the abolitionist cause in his speeches and articles.[15]

H. Bruce Franklin has called the slave narrative the first distinctively American literary genre.[16] Several dozen slave narratives had been published in North America before the appearance of Douglass's first autobiography, and altogether two hundred have been identified as having been issued and reissued during and after the period of legal slavery in the United States. This includes two more autobiographies by Frederick Douglass—*My Bondage and My Freedom* and *The Life and Times of Frederick Douglass*—as well as multiple autobiographies by other authors.

The earliest example of the genre is Olaudah Equiano's *Interesting Narrative of the Life of Olaudah Equiano*. Others include Nat Turner's *Confessions*, Moses Grandy's *Narrative of the Life of Moses Grandy, Late a Slave in the United States of America*, Henry Box Brown's *Narrative of Henry Box Brown, Who Escaped from Slavery Enclosed in a Box 3 Feet Long and*

2 *Wide,* and Booker T. Washington's well-known *Up From Slavery.* As many feminist scholars have remarked, the slave narrative as genre is thoroughly gendered. Not only were few narratives produced by women—one thinks of Sojourner's Truth's *Narrative,* but most important Harriet Jacobs' *Incidents in the Life of a Slave Girl*—they also disclosed the way gender structured the telling of stories about slavery. Jacobs' *Incidents,* for example, reveals that she both sustained and worked against the influence of the sentimental novel of the era. She closed her book with an address to her readership that reminded them that her objective was liberation and therefore did not conform to the conventional denouement of sentimental novels and the anticipated aspirations of white women: "Reader, my story ends with freedom; not in the usual way with marriage."[17]

Of the countless editions of Douglass's *Narrative* that have been published over the last fifty years, some have attempted to help us grasp the gendered framework of his story—and, by extension, of the genre itself. Random House published Douglass's *Narrative* and Jacobs' *Incidents in the Life of a Slave Girl* together in a Modern Library Classic edition in 2000 with an introduction by Kwame Anthony Appiah. Highlighting the role Douglass's violated masculinity plays in shaping his conceptualization of freedom, Appiah points out that "the driving energy of the book is Douglass's need to live not just as a free person, but as a free *man.* And he becomes a man . . . in part by besting another white man—Covey the slave-breaker—in a fight."[18] What is not so clear in Appiah's claim that for Harriet Jacobs, the author of the narrative accompanying Douglass's, "the escape from slavery was a search for life not just as a free person, but as a free woman,"[19] is that lurking within the definition of black freedom as the reclamation of black manhood is the obligatory suppression of black womanhood.

Deborah McDowell provided an insightful introduction to the Oxford University Press's 1999 edition of Douglass's *Narrative* in which she called attention to the patriarchal assumptions in the text. Any reader of Douglass's autobiographies—whether the *Narrative, My Bondage and My Freedom,* or *The Life and Times of Frederick Douglass*—is familiar with the gripping scene of Douglass battling the slave-breaker Covey. Douglass wrote that in the period preceding the battle,

> Mr. Covey succeeded in breaking me. I was broken in body, soul, and spirit. My natural elasticity was crushed, my intellect languished, the disposition to read departed, the cheerful spark that lingered above my eye died; the dark night of slavery closed in upon me; and behold a man transformed into a brute![20]

His later description of the fight with Covey is prefaced by this message to the reader: "You have seen how a man was made a slave: you shall now see how a slave was made a man."[21] According to McDowell, the aim of this passage is:

> . . . to underscore that "slave" and "man" are as mutual-
> ly contradictory as "American" and "slave" . . . Douglass
> . . . leaves untouched the structuring opposition: male
> and female, for subject and object are thoroughly and
> conventionally gendered throughout the *Narrative*. In
> other words, inasmuch as "manhood" and "freedom"
> function throughout Douglass's discourse on slavery as
> coincident terms, his journey from slavery to freedom
> leaves women in the logical position of representing the
> condition of slavery. Douglass's refusal to be whipped
> represents not only an assertion of manhood but the
> transcendence of slavery, an option his *Narrative* denies
> to women.[22]

One of the implications of the definition of "freedom" in terms of "manhood" is that the closest black women can come to freedom is to achieve the status not of a free man, but rather the unliberated status of the white woman. Harriet Jacobs may well have been intentionally troubling this idea when she decided to draw attention to the fact that her book closes with the attainment of "freedom" rather than "marriage."

McDowell makes the point that in Douglass's *Narrative*, maimed, flogged, abused black female bodies are the anchors of his description of slavery.[23] "The *Narrative*," she writes, "is literally populated with the whipped bodies of slave women."[24] One of McDowell's references is to the beating of Aunt Hester, which Douglass describes at the very beginning of his book. ("I have often been awakened at the dawn of day by the most heart-rending shrieks of an own aunt of mine, whom he [the overseer] used to tie up to a joist, and whip upon her naked back till she was literally covered with blood.")[25] This was what Douglass referred to as "the blood-stained gate, the entrance to the hell of slavery."[26]

Of course Frederick Douglass was not alone in his evocation of women's bodies as objects of slavery's appalling violence, and it would be unfair to single him out individually for using this convention or for failing to apprehend how literary representations of black women's bodies as targets of slavery's most horrific forms of violence might also tend to objectify slave women and discursively deprive them of the capacity to strike out for their own freedom. Abolitionists—both black and white—were well aware of the way audiences could be expected to respond to evocations of slavery's violences against women and thus frequently used examples similar to those in the *Narrative*. They also assumed that emancipation from slavery would entail in the first place, freedom for black men. Moreover, they assumed that the violent repression of black women was indirectly an attack on black men, who were not allowed to protect "their" women in the way white men might be expected to protect "theirs."

As twenty-first-century readers, our historical vantage point can be more complex and our reading can be more nuanced. Just as we know and applaud the accomplishments of the nineteenth-century Women's Rights movement, while recognizing that despite the best intentions of its participants, the movement was thoroughly saturated with racism, we are also able to hold Frederick Douglass in the highest regard, while also acknowledging his and his era's inability to imagine the full equality of women—especially those women who were subjugated by virtue of race and gender.

McDowell's analysis does not in any sense diminish the significance of Frederick Douglass's work. Indeed, even though he, like all of his contemporaries, was a product of his times, and was shaped by many of the prevailing ideological assumptions, he was able, more than most, to critically apprehend the fallacious ideologies justifying black inferiority and women's inferiority. As McDowell emphatically points out, Douglass played the most prominent role among all the men present at the first women's rights conference in Seneca Falls, New York, in 1848 and chose as a slogan for his newspaper "Right is of no sex—Truth is of no color."[27] Yet, it could not be expected of him to recognize all of the ramifications of the male supremacist ideas that permeated the institutional and ideological landscapes of his time. Thus, even as McDowell critiques what she perceives to be a rhetorical exploitation of the black female body, she also highlights the important role Douglass played in the nascent Women's Rights movement. The edition of the *Narrative* for which McDowell provides an introduction also includes several articles from Douglass's newspaper urging the public to support women's rights, including woman suffrage.

When I first read Douglass's *Narrative*, I had not yet learned how to recognize the extent to which the equivalence of "freedom" and "manhood" meant that women were excluded by definition from enjoying the full benefits of freedom. In fact, today I find it simultaneously somewhat embarrassing to realize that my UCLA lectures on Douglass rely on an implicitly masculinist notion of freedom, and exciting to realize how much we have matured with respect to feminist analysis since that period. Thanks to my training in German philosophy, I had acquired conceptual tools that allowed me to analyze the complex trajectories from bondage to freedom (using, for example Hegel's approach to the relationship between master and slave in *The Phenomenology of Mind,*), but it was not until I began to work on "The Black Women's Role in the Community of Slaves" (a year later during the time I was imprisoned) that I began to recognize the fundamental importance of developing gender analyses.

As I revisit the lectures that accompany this current edition of Frederick Douglass's *Narrative*, I am surprised by how much I did not know at the beginning of an era that witnessed the rise of Black Studies and Women's/Feminist Studies. In 1969, when I was hired by UCLA's Department of Philosophy to teach courses in Continental Philosophy, I welcomed the opportunity to teach courses in the tradition forged by Kant, Hegel, and Marx. Such courses would allow me to put to good use my training as a student of Herbert Marcuse and Theodor Adorno. But I was also deeply interested in the emergence of Black Studies—at UCLA, the Center for Afro-American Studies was founded shortly before I joined the Philosophy faculty—and wanted my teaching to incorporate these new developments. At that time there was no available body of literature on black philosophy, nor was there a significant group of philosophy scholars who worked on issues of race and ethnicity. Consequently I decided to design a course that I called "Recurring Philosophical Themes in Black Literature" that would entail examining black literary texts with the aim of identifying the major philosophical questions they posed.

The overarching question I considered in the course was that of liberation. I intended to think about liberation both in broad philosophical terms and in the way the theme of liberation is embedded in the literary history of black people in North America. Although current events were beyond the scope of the course, I expected the students to take note of the wide-ranging engagements with theories and practices of liberation in movement circles. After all, it was 1969, barely a year and a half since the assassination of Dr. Martin Luther King, which had rekindled popular discussion and organizing around strategies of liberation. Internecine strife within the black youth movement pitted cultural nationalists against socialists and internationalists, and it had been a little less than a year since Black Panther leaders John Huggins and Bunchy Carter were killed by members of the cultural nationalist association known as US Organization during a Black Student Union meeting on the UCLA campus. Moreover, I, myself, had been under intense political pressure since California Governor Ronald Reagan and the Regents of the University of California had announced shortly before I began to teach that they were firing me because of my membership in the Communist Party USA. I taught this course on philosophy and black literature while seeking and eventually receiving a court ruling enjoining the Regents from firing me based on my political affiliation.

I should point out that even though there was no formal incorporation of gender analyses into my first courses, my activist experiences involved intense battles over the role of women in such black community organizations as the Student Nonviolent Coordinating Committee and the Black Panther Party. The patriarchal structure of the cultural nationalist US Organization left no space for contestation. Moreover, I had personally come under attack by some members of the community who did not think that I deserved to take a leadership position given the fact that I was a woman.

The approach to the question of liberation I pursued in "Recurring Philosophical Themes in Black Literature" linked philosophical understandings of freedom with histories of

black political struggle and cultural production as they resonated with contemporary efforts to extend and enlarge the
meaning of freedom. What better text to begin with than
Frederick Douglass's autobiography? Students would follow
a trajectory from bondage to liberty that would help them to
better apprehend the nature of freedom as forged by those
who have had most at stake in the struggle for liberation.
The first two lectures—based on rough transcripts of my remarks, which referred to the later autobiography, *The Life
and Times of Frederick Douglass*—accompany this edition of
Frederick Douglass's *Narrative*. They are published here in
the form in which they were circulated in 1970 after I was
arrested on charges of murder, kidnapping, and conspira-
cy, which included a strong letter of support from faculty
members at UCLA. When I taught this course, I did not realize that less than a year later, I would be in jail awaiting
trial on what were initially three capital charges.

In the 1960s and '70s, the perceived urgency of the political moment led many readers of Douglass's narrative to
reflect on the prospects of liberation in the twentieth century as they read about his quest for freedom in the nine
teenth. Douglass's status as the preeminent voice of the
black anti-slavery movement led many people to search his
writings for clues about how to conduct twentieth-century
liberation struggles. One of the most recognizable passages
from his writings, which continues to be frequently quoted
today, comes from a speech he delivered in August 1857 on

the occasion of West India Emancipation Day, marking the twenty-third anniversary of the abolition of the slave trade in Britain.

If there is no struggle there is no progress. Those who profess to favor freedom and yet deprecate agitation are men who want crops without plowing up the ground; they want rain without thunder and lightning. They want the ocean without the awful roar of its many waters.

This struggle may be a moral one, or it may be a physical one, and it may be both moral and physical, but it must be a struggle. Power concedes nothing without a demand. It never did and it never will. Find out just what any people will quietly submit to and you have found out the exact measure of injustice and wrong which will be imposed upon them, and these will continue till they are resisted with either words or blows, or with both. The limits of tyrants are prescribed by the endurance of those whom they oppress. In the light of these ideas, Negroes will be hunted at the North and held and flogged at the South so long as they submit to those devilish outrages and make no resistance, either moral or physical. Men may not get all they pay for in this world, but they must certainly pay for all they get. If we ever get free from the oppressions and wrongs heaped upon us, we must pay for their removal. We must do this by labor, by suffering, by sacrifice, and if needs be, by our lives and the lives of others.[28]

This message resonated with activists and supporters of

the various liberation movements of the 1960s—from the African, Asian, and Latin American liberation movements to the movements inside the United States that called for a definitive end to racism.

Given that Douglass's insistence that progress always requires struggle and that freedom must be fought for and won, not offered as a gift, has, in fact, been repeated often by movements since the 1960s, it should be possible to make fresh connections with Douglass's life and works today.

What, then, might be the resonance of Douglass's writings—and the *Narrative*, in particular—as we experience the first administration of the first African American president of the United States? Barack Obama certainly posited a connection between Douglass's political quest and his own. In a number of campaign speeches, he made implicit references to Douglass's words, often emphasizing that "power concedes nothing without a fight," and, referring in his victory speech, for example, to "struggles and progress" over the last decades.

Intriguingly, I write this introduction as President Obama returns from his first official trip to Ghana, during which he and the First Family visited Cape Coast Castle. The media coverage of his family's encounter with the historical African slave trade—including a walk through the tunnel at the end of which was the door of no return—has spun multiple ruminations on slavery, including an inquiry into Michelle Obama's slave past. Coincidentally, shortly before the Obamas traveled to Ghana, the U.S. Senate passed a resolution delivering an official apology for slavery, concurring with House resolution of 2008. (At the same time, the U.S. government—along with other Western governments—boycotted the 2009 World Conference Against Racism, thus failing to recognize the links between slavery, colonization and the current sitution of the Palestinians.)

How then do we read Douglass's narrative today? How do we think about slavery's inheritances that continue to shape contemporary institutions and practices? What have we learned in the many years since the first publication of the *Narrative* that might assist us in developing richer, more layered, more complicated readings of this text on slavery, resistance, and liberation? What, for example can we say about the obsession with black women as objects of the most unspeakable forms of violence? In assenting to the critiques proposed by feminist scholars, we also recognize that portrayals of suffering black women were widely used to convey the horrors of slavery. Because of prevailing hierarchies of gender—which also influenced black people—the suffering woman was interpreted as an implicit assault on the black man. The instrumentality of violence against enslaved women was such that it could be materially effective in maintaining the system, but it was also ideologically effective in sustaining gendered hierarchies of power even in black abolitionist circles.

Thus, in criticizing the text's abundance of images of

enslaved, thrashed, and battered black women, we should not read these images as needing to be excised from the *Narrative*, but rather we should try to develop a framework that foregrounds both the complexities of gendered violence under slavery and possible gendered strategies for freedom. We might begin by examining the instrumentality of slavery's gendered violences, which were not the product of inherently evil individual actors, but rather were designed to further the system of slavery itself. In numerous slave narratives, we discover descriptions of special forms of punishment relegated to pregnant women, who could be compelled to lie down over a hole in the ground designed to "protect" the pregnancy as the slave-owner's future property, while an overseer flogged them. Moses Grandy's words indicate that the violence was such that it sometimes exceeded its own purpose and led to the death of both mother and fetus.

> A woman who gives offense in the field, and is large in a family way, is compelled to lie down over a hole made to receive her corpulency, and is flogged with the whip or beat with a paddle, which has holes in it; at ever stroke comes a blister. One of my sisters was so severely punished in this way that labor was brought on, and the child was born in the field. This very overseer, Mr. Brooks, killed in this manner a girl named Mary. [29]

At the same time we should not be so overwhelmed by the enormity of this violence that we forget that its target is a subject who deserves to be free. In other words, we should not allow such emotions as pity to foreclose possibilities of solidarity. Real stories today of the sexual coercion and abuse of women prisoners reveal the inheritances of slavery and our responses often recapitulate those of nineteenth-century abolitionists.

How, then, can we read Douglass's *Narrative* in a way that will help us to understand slavery as Douglass experienced it and to understand the legacies of slavery as they are crystallized today in multiple regimes of violence against women and men? Moreover, what are the links between modes of institutional violence—such as that inflicted on women in prison—and the pandemic of intimate, domestic, individual violence against women? Understanding the inheritances of slavery helps us to better grasp the complex challenges of the present.

Theories of liberation during the 1960s and '70s, as important as they were at the time, failed to grasp the extent to which slavery left indelible marks on both institutional and individual practices. Many of us thought that liberation was simply a question of organizing to leverage power from the hands of those we deemed to be the oppressors. Frederick Douglass certainly helped us to conceptualize this, but this was not, by far, the complete story. Today readers of Douglass, scholars and activists alike, do his text justice by bringing a much more expansive sense of what it means to struggle for liberation, one that embraces not only women of color, but also sexually marginalized communities as well as those subject to modes of containment and repression by virtue of their resident status as immigrants. Equally important, as we recognize the extent to which Douglass sustained the influence of the ideologies of his era, we might better learn how to identify and struggle with those that limit our imagination of liberation today.

—Angela Y. Davis
July 2009

LECTURES ON LIBERATION

LECTURES ON LIBERATION

Introduction to the 1970 pamphlet published by the
N.Y. Committee to Free Angela Davis

By UCLA Professors

Presented here are Professor Angela Davis's initial lectures for "Recurring Philosophical Themes in Black Literature," her first course at UCLA, taught during the Fall Quarter of 1969. At the time she was beginning a two-year appointment as Acting Assistant Professor in Philosophy, an appointment duly recommended by the Department of Philosophy and enthusiastically approved by the UCLA administration. The first of the two lectures was delivered in Royce Hall to an audience of over fifteen hundred students and interested colleagues. At the lecture's end Professor Davis was given a prolonged standing ovation by the audience. It was, we thought, a vindication of academic freedom and democratic education. For the lectures are a part of an attempt to bring to light the forbidden history of the enslavement and oppression of black people, and to place that history in an illuminating philosophical context. At the same time, they are sensitive, original and incisive; the work of an excellent teacher and a truly fine scholar.

Now Professor Davis is a prisoner of the society that should have welcomed her talents, her honesty and the contribution she was making toward understanding and resolving the most critical problem of that society—the division between its oppressors and its oppressed. First she was attacked by the Regents of the University of California, who attempted to dismiss her from the University on the patently illegal ground of her membership in the Communist Party. When this attempt was overruled by the Superior Court of Los Angeles, the Regents denied her the normal continuation of her appointment for a second year, in spite of recommendations from a host of review committees and the Chancellor of UCLA that she be reappointed. During the summer of 1970, she was charged with kidnapping, murder, and unlawful flight to avoid prosecution, and was placed on the FBI most wanted list. When apprehended, she was held on excessive bail, then denied bail, and subsequently has been kept in isolation from other prisoners.

In her first lecture Professor Davis points out that keeping an oppressed class in ignorance is one of the principal instruments of its oppression. Like Frederick Douglass, the black slave whose life and work she surveys here, Professor Davis is one of the educated oppressed. Like him, she has achieved full consciousness of what it is to be oppressed, and has heightened this consciousness in her own people and in others. There can be little doubt that her effectiveness in blunting the oppressive weapon of ignorance was the chief motive for her removal from the University of California, and a major motive in the harsh treatment she has since received.

These are lectures dealing with the phenomenology of oppression and liberation. It is one thing to make the elementary point that millions are still oppressed in what is advertised as the world's most free society. It is much more difficult to lay out the causes of that oppression and the ways in which it is perpetuated; its psychological meaning to the oppressor and the oppressed; and the process by which the latter becomes conscious of it; and the way in which they triumph over it. This was the task Professor Davis set for herself. She brings to her work a rich philosophical background, a piercing intellect, and the knowledge born of experience.

It was perhaps inevitable that Professor Davis should become a symbol for conflicting groups and causes. But it is well to remember that behind the symbol lies the human being whose thoughts are recorded here, and that when she stands trial not only a human cause but also a human life will be tried. In the meantime, we take pride in presenting these two lectures by a distinguished colleague and friend. May they everywhere contribute to the defeat of oppression.

Signed,
Matthew Skulicz, English
Peter Orleans, Sociology
David Gillman, Mathematics

Sterling Robbins, Anthropology
Marie Brand, Nursing
J.C. Ries, Political Science
Jerome Rabow, Sociology
Donald Kalish, Philosophy
Evelyn Hatch, English
Kenneth Chapman, German
Laurence Morrissette, French
Temma Kaplan, History
Peter Ladefoged, Linguistics
D.R. McCann, German
Robert Singleton, Business Administration
Richard Ashcraft, Political Science
John Horton, Sociology
Paul Koosis, Mathematics
Patrick Story, English
Alan E. Flanigan, Engineering
Roy L. Wolford, Medicine
Albert Schwartz, History
Wade Savage, Philosophy
Tom Robinson, Education
Barbara Partee, English
Carlos Otero, Spanish
Alex Norman, Urban Affairs
Henry McGee, School of Law
E.V. Wolfenstein, Political Science

The idea of freedom has justifiably been a dominating theme in the history of Western ideas. Man has been repeatedly defined in terms of his inalienable freedom. One of the most acute paradoxes present in the history of Western society is that while on a philosophical plane freedom has been delineated in the most lofty and sublime fashion, concrete reality has always been permeated with the most brutal forms of unfreedom, of enslavement. In ancient Greece where, so we are taught, democracy had its source, it cannot be overlooked that in spite of all the philosophical assertions of man's freedom, in spite of the demand that man realize himself through exercising his freedom as a citizen of the polis, the majority of the people in Athens were not free. Women were not citizens and slavery was an accepted institution. Moreover, there was definitely a form of racism present in Greek society, for only Greeks were suited for the benefits of freedom: all non-Greeks were called barbarians and by their very nature could not be deserving or even capable of freedom.

In this context, one cannot fail to conjure up the image of Thomas Jefferson and the other so-called Founding Fathers formulating the noble concepts of the Constitution of the United States while their slaves were living in misery. In order not to mar the beauty of the Constitution and at the same time to protect the institution of slavery, they wrote about "persons held to service or labor," a euphemism for the word slavery, as being exceptional types of human beings, persons who do not merit the guarantees and rights of the Constitution.

Is man free or is he not? Ought he be free or ought not he be free? The history of Black literature provides, in my opinion, a much more illuminating account of the nature of freedom, its extent and limits, than all the philosophical discourses on this theme in the history of Western society. Why? For a number of reasons. First of all, because Black literature in this country and throughout the world projects the consciousness of a people who have been denied entrance into the real world of freedom. Black people have exposed, by their very existence, the inadequacies not only of the practice of freedom, but of its very theoretical formulation. Because, if the theory of freedom remains isolated from the practice of freedom or rather is contradicted in reality, then this means that something must be wrong with the concept—that is, if we are thinking in a dialectical manner.

The pivotal theme of this course will thus be the idea of freedom as it is unfolded in the literary understanding of Black people. Starting with Frederick Douglass we will explore the slave's experience of his bondage and thus the negative experience of freedom. Most important here will be the crucial transformation of the concept of freedom as a static, given principle into the concept of liberation, the dynamic, active struggle for freedom. We will move on to W. E. B. DuBois, to Jean Tommer, Richard Wright and John A. Williams. Interspersed will be poetry from the various periods of Black History in this country, and theoretical analyses such as Fanon and DuBois' *A. B. C. of Color*. Finally I would like to discuss a few pieces by African writers and poems by Nicolás Guillén, a Black Cuban poet, and compare them to the work of American Blacks.

Throughout the course, I have said, the notion of freedom will be the axis around which we will attempt to develop other philosophical concepts. We will encounter such metaphysical notions as identity, the problem of self-knowledge. The kind of philosophy of history that emerges out of the works we are studying will be crucial. The morality peculiar to an oppressed people is something we will have to come to grips with. As we progress along the path of the unfolding of freedom in Black literature, we should retrieve a whole host of related themes.

Before I get into the material, I would like to say a few words about the kinds of questions we ought to ask ourselves when we delve into the nature of human freedom. First of all, is freedom totally subjective, totally objective, or is it a synthesis of both poles? Let me try to explain what I mean. Is freedom to be conceived merely as an inherent, given characteristic of man, is it a freedom that is confined within the human mind, is freedom an internal experience? Or, on the other hand, is freedom only the liberty to move, to act in a way one chooses? Let us pose the original question as to the subjectivity or objectivity of freedom in the following manner: Is freedom the freedom of thought or the freedom of action? Or more important, is it possible to conceive of the one without the other?

This leads us directly to the problem of whether freedom is at all possible within the bounds of material bondage. Can the slave be said to be free in any way? This brings to mind one of the more notorious statements that the French existentialist Jean-Paul Sartre has made. Even the man in chains, he says, remains free, and for this reason: he is always at liberty to eliminate his condition of slavery even if this means his death. That is, his freedom is narrowly defined as the freedom to choose between his state of captivity and his death. This is extreme. But we have to decide whether or not this is the way in which we are going to define that concept. Certainly, this would not be compatible with the notion of liberation, for when the slave opts for death, he does much more than obliterate his condition of enslavement, for at the same time he is abolishing the very condition of freedom, life. Yet there is more to be said, when we take the decision to die out of an abstract context and examine the dynamics of a real situation in which a slave meets his death in the fight for concrete freedom. That is to say, the choice, slavery or death, could either mean slavery or suicide, or on the other hand, slavery or liberation at all costs. The difference between the two situations is crucial.

The collective consciousness of an oppressed people entails an understanding of the conditions of oppression and the possibilities of abolishing these conditions. At the end of his journey towards understanding, the slave finds a real grasp of what freedom means. He knows that it means the destruction of the master-slave relationship. And in this sense, his knowledge of freedom is more profound than that of the master. For the master feels himself free and he feels himself free because he is able to control the lives of others. He is free at the expense of the freedom of another. The slave experiences the freedom of the master in its true light. He understands that the master's freedom is abstract freedom to suppress other human beings. The slave understands that this is a pseudo concept of freedom and at this point is more enlightened than his master for he realizes that the master is a slave of his own misconceptions, his own misdeeds, his own brutality, his own effort to oppress.

Now I would like to go into the material. *Narrative of the Life of Frederick Douglass* constitutes a physical voyage from slavery to freedom that is both the conclusion and reflection of a philosophical voyage from slavery to freedom. We will see that neither voyage would have been possible alone; they are mutually determinant.

The point of departure for this voyage is the exclamation Frederick Douglass makes as a child, "O God, save me!

God, deliver me! Let me be free! Is there any God? Why am I a slave? I will run away. I will not stand it. Get caught, or get clear, I'll try it. . . . It cannot be that I will live and die a slave."[30] His critical attitude when he fails to accept the usual answer—that God had made Black people to be slaves and white people to be masters—is the basic condition that must be present before freedom can become a possibility in the mind of the slave. We must not forget that throughout the history of Western society there is an abundance of justifications for the existence of slavery. Both Plato and Aristotle felt that some men were born to be slaves, some men are not born into a state of freedom. Religious justifications for slavery are to be found at every turn.

Let's attempt to arrive at a philosophical definition of the slave. We have already stated the essence: he is a human being who, by some reason or another, is denied freedom. But is not the essence of the human being his freedom? Either the slave is not a man or his very existence is a contradiction. We can rule out the first alternative, although we should not forget that the prevailing ideology defined the Black man as subhuman. The failure to deal with the contradictory nature of slavery, the imposed ignorance of reality is exemplified in the notion that the slave is not a man, for if he were a man, he should certainly be free.

We all know of the calculated attempts to rob the Black man of his humanity. We know that in order to maintain the institution of slavery, black people were forced to live in conditions not fit for animals. The white slave-owners were determined to mould Black people into the image of the subhuman being which they had contrived in order to justify their actions. A vicious circle emerges in which the slave-owner loses all consciousness of himself.

The vicious circle continues to turn, but for the slave, there is a way out: Resistance. Frederick Douglass had one of his first experiences of this possibility of a slave becoming free upon resisting his own whipping:

> Covey at length let me go, puffing and blowing at a great rate, saying that if I had not resisted, he would not have whipped me half so much. The truth was, that he had not whipped me at all. . . . This battle with Mr. Covey was the turning-point in my career as a slave. It rekindled the few expiring embers of freedom, and revived within me a sense of my own manhood. It recalled the departed self-confidence, and inspired me again with a determination to be free. The gratification afforded by the triumph was a full compensation for whatever else might follow, even death itself. He can only understand the deep satisfaction which I experienced, who has himself repelled by force the bloody arm of slavery. I felt as I never felt before. It was a glorious resurrection, from the tomb of slavery, to the heaven of freedom. My long-crushed spirit rose, cowardice departed, bold defiance took its place; and I now resolved that, however long I might remain a slave in form, the day passed forever when I could be a slave in fact. I did not hesitate to let it be known of me,

that the white man who expected to succeed in whipping, must also succeed in killing me."[31]

Already we can begin to concretize the notion of freedom as it appeared to the slave. The first condition of freedom is the open act of resistance—physical resistance, violent resistance. In that act of resistance, the rudiments of freedom are already present. And the violent retaliation signifies much more than the physical act: it is refusal not only to submit to the flogging, but refusal to accept the definitions of the slavemaster; it is implicitly a rejection of the institution of slavery, its standards, its morality, a microcosmic effort towards liberation. Douglass later wrote, "That slave who had the courage to stand up for himself against the overseer, although he might have hard stripes at first, became while legally a slave virtually a free man."[32]

The slave is actually conscious of the fact that freedom is not a fact, it is not a given, but rather something to be fought for; it can exist only through a process of struggle. The slavemaster, on the other hand, experiences his freedom as inalienable and thus as a fact: he is not aware that he too has been enslaved by his own system.

To begin to answer a question we posed earlier—is it possible for a man to be in chains and at the same time be free— we can now say that the path towards freedom can only be envisioned by the slave when he actively rejects his chains. The first phase of liberation is the decision to reject the image of himself that the slave-owner has painted, to reject the conditions that the slave-owner has created, to reject his own existence, to reject himself as slave.

Here the problem of freedom leads us directly into the question of identity. The condition of slavery is a condition of alienation. In a later autobiography he wrote, "Nature never intended that men and women should be either slaves or slaveholders, and nothing but rigid training long persisted in, can perfect the character of the one or the other." Slavery is an alienation from a natural condition, it is a violation of nature that distorts both parties—the slave and the slave-owner. Alienation is the absence of authentic identity, in the case of the slave, he is alienated from his own freedom.

This non-identity can exist on a number of levels: it can be unconscious—the slave accepts the master's definition, renders himself *unfree* in seeing himself as inherently unfit for freedom. Or it can be conscious, knowledge can strike a blow at it. We are most concerned with the second alternative, for it constitutes a stage in the voyage towards freedom.

The most extreme form of human alienation is the reduction to the status of property. This is how the slave was defined: something to be owned.

> We were all ranked together at the valuation. Men and women, old and young, married and single, were ranked with horses, sheep, and swine. There were horses and

53

men, cattle and women, pigs and children, all holding
the same rank in the scale of being, and were all subjected to the same narrow examination. Silvery-headed age
and sprightly youth, maids and matrons, had to undergo
the same indelicate inspection. At this moment, I saw
more clearly than ever the brutalizing effects of slavery
upon both slave and slaveholder.[33]

Black people were treated as things, they were defined as
objects. "The slave was a fixture," Douglass later remarked.
His life must be lived within the limits of that objectness,
within the limits of the white man's definition of the Black
man. Forced to live as if he were a fixture, the slave's perception of the world is inverted. Because his life is relegated to
that of an object, he must forge his own humanity within
those boundaries. "We had no more voice in that decision
than the brutes among whom we were ranked."[34] The slave
has no determination whatsoever over the external circumstances of his life. One day a woman could be living
on a plantation among her children, their father—family,
friends. The next day, she could be miles away with no hope
of ever meeting them again. The idea of the journey loses its
connotation of exploration, it loses the excitement of learning the unknown. The trip becomes a journey into hell, not
away from the thingness of the slave's existence, but an even
sharper accentuation of his non-human external existence.
"A single word from the white men was enough—against all
our wishes, prayers, and entreaties—to sunder forever the

dearest friends, dearest kindred, and strongest ties known to human beings."[35] Frederick Douglass gives a moving account of the last days of his grandmother, who having faithfully served her master from his birth to his death, having had children and grandchildren for him, is looked upon in disdain by her then present owner—the original master's grandson. She is sent into the woods to die a solitary death.

Frederick Douglass's owner reveals to him unwittingly the path toward the consciousness of his alienation: "'If you give a nigger an inch, he will take an ell. A nigger should know nothing but to obey his master—to do as he is told to do. Learning would spoil the best nigger in the world. Now,' said he, 'if you teach that nigger (speaking of myself) how to read, there would be no keeping him. It would forever unfit him to be a slave. He would at once become unmanageable, and of no value to his master. As to himself, it could do him no good, but a great deal of harm. It would make him discontented and unhappy.'"[36] The slave is alienated totally insofar as he accepts his master's will as the absolute authority over his life. The slave has no will, no desires, no being—his essence, his being he must find entirely in the will of his master. What does this mean? It is partly with the slave's consent that the white man is able to perpetuate slavery—when we say consent, however, it is not free consent, but consent under the most brutal force and pressure.

Frederick Douglass learns from his owner's observations precisely how he is to combat his own alienation: "I now

understood what had been to me a most perplexing difficulty—to wit, the white man's power to enslave a black man.
It was a grand achievement, and I prized it highly. From that
moment, I understood the pathway from slavery to freedom."[37] If we look closely at the words of Frederick Douglass
we can detect the theme of resistance once again. His first
concrete experience of the possibility of freedom within
the limits of slavery comes when he observes a slave resist
a whipping. Now he transforms this resistance into a resistance of the mind, a refusal to accept the will of the master
and a determination to find independent means of judging
the world.

Just as the slave has used violence against the violence
of the aggressor, Frederick Douglass uses the knowledge of
his owner, i.e., that learning unfits a man to be a slave and
turns it against him: he will set out to acquire knowledge,
precisely because it unfits a man to be a slave. Resistance, rejection, on every level, on every front, are integral elements
of the voyage towards freedom. Alienation will become conscious through the process of knowledge.

In combating his ignorance, in resisting the will of his
master, Frederick Douglass apprehends that all men should
be free, and thus deepens his knowledge of slavery, of what
it means to be a slave, what it means to be the negative
counterpart of freedom, "I would sometimes say to them, I
wished I could be as free as they would be when they got to
be men. 'You will be free as soon as you are twenty-one, but I

am a slave for life! Have not I as good a right to be free as you have?' These words used to trouble them; they would express for me the liveliest sympathy, and console me with the hope that something would occur by which I might be free. I was now about twelve years old, and the thought of being a slave for life began to bear heavily upon my heart."[38]

His alienation becomes real, it surfaces, and Frederick Douglass is going to existentially experience all that is entailed by being bound to a state of unfreedom materially, while mentally finding his way toward liberation. The tension between the subjective and the objective will eventually provide the impetus towards total liberation. But before that goal is reached a whole series of phases must be traversed.

The slave, Frederick Douglass, thus mentally transcends his condition towards freedom. Herein lies the consciousness of alienation. He sees freedom concretely as the negation of his condition—it is present in the very air he breathes.

> As I read and contemplated the subject, behold! that very discontentment which Master Hugh had predicted would follow my learning to read had already come, to torment and sting my soul to unutterable anguish. As I writhed under it, I would at times feel that learning to read had been a curse rather than a blessing. It had given me a view of my wretched condition, without the remedy. It opened my eyes to the horrible pit, but to no ladder upon which to get out. In moments of agony, I

envied my fellow-slaves for their stupidity. I have often
wished myself a beast. I preferred the condition of the
meanest reptile to my own. Anything, no matter what,
to get rid of thinking! It was this everlasting thinking of
my condition that tormented me. There was no getting
rid of it. It was pressed upon me by every object within
sight or hearing, animate or inanimate. The silver trump
of freedom had roused my soul to eternal wakefulness.
Freedom now appeared, to disappear no more forever. It
was heard in every sound, and seen in every thing. It was
ever present to torment me with a sense of my wretched
condition. I saw nothing without seeing it, I heard nothing without hearing it, and felt nothing without feeling it. It looked from every star, it smiled in every calm,
breathed in every wind, and moved in every storm.[39]

He has arrived at a true recognition of his condition. That
recognition is at the same time the rejection of that condition. Consciousness of alienation entails the absolute refusal to accept that alienation. But the slave's predicament, by
its very contradictory nature, is impossible: enlightenment
does not bring happiness, nor does it bring real freedom—it
brings desolation, misery, i.e., as long as the slave does not
see a concrete path out of enslavement. In speaking of the
slave-owner's wife, Frederick Douglass says: "If I was in a
separate room any considerable length of time, I was sure
to be suspected of having a book, and was at once called
to give an account of myself. Mistress, in teaching me the

alphabet, had given me the *inch*, and no precaution could prevent me from taking the *ell*."[40]

Moreover, it is not just his individual condition that the slave rejects, and thus his misery is not just a result of his individual unfreedom, his individual alienation. True consciousness is the rejection of the institution itself and everything that accompanies it. "It was slavery and not its mere incidents that I hated," he later wrote.[41] To foreshadow Frederick Douglass's path from slavery to freedom, even when he attains his own freedom, he does not see the real goal as having been attained. It is only with the total abolition of the *institution* of slavery that his misery, his desolation, his alienation will be eliminated. And not even then, for there will remain remnants and there still remain in existence today the causes that gave rise to slavery.

On this road to freedom, Frederick Douglass experiences religion as a reinforcement and justification for his desire to be free. Out of the Christian doctrine, he deduces the equality of all men before God. If this is true, he infers, then slavemasters must be defying the will of God by suppressing the will of human beings and should be dealt with in accordance with God's anger. Freedom, the abolition of slavery, liberation, the destruction of alienation—these notions receive a metaphysical justification and impetus through religion. A supernatural being wills the abolition of slavery: Frederick Douglass, slave and believer in God, must accomplish God's will by working towards the goal of liberation.

Douglass was not the only person to infer this from the Christian religion. Nat Turner received an important part of his inspiration from his faith in Christianity. John Brown was another example.

We all know that from the perspective of white, slave-owning society, Christianity was supposed to serve quite another function. The overriding idea behind exposing the slaves to religion was to provide a metaphysical justification, not for freedom, but rather for slavery.

One of Karl Marx's more notorious statements is that religion is the opium of the people. That is—religion teaches men to be satisfied with their condition in this world—with their oppression—by directing their hopes and desires into a supernatural domain. A little suffering during a person's existence in this world means nothing compared to an eternity of bliss.

Marcuse likes to point out that we often ignore the fact that Karl Marx also said that religion is the wish-dream of an oppressed humanity. On the one hand this statement means, of course, that wishes become dreams projected into an imaginary realm. But on the other hand, we have to ask ourselves: is there anything else implied in Marx's statement about the notion of wish-dreams of an oppressed humanity? Think for a moment. Real wants, needs and desires are transformed into wish-dreams via the process of religion, because it seems so hopeless in this world: this is the perspective of an oppressed people. But what is important, what is crucial is that those dreams are always on the verge of reverting to their original status—the real wishes and needs here on Earth. There is always the possibility of redirecting those wish-dreams to the here-and-now.

Frederick Douglass redirected those dreams. Nat Turner placed them within the framework of the real world. So there can be a positive function of religion because its very nature is to satisfy very urgent needs of people who are oppressed. (We are speaking only of the relation of oppressed people to religion, not attempting to analyze the notion of religion in and for itself.) There can be a positive function of religion. All that need be done is to say: let's begin to create that eternity of bliss for human society here in this world. Let's convert eternity into history.

Why is it that more Black people did not shift the emphasis from the other world to concrete reality—to history? There was a calculated effort on the part of white, slave-owning society to create a special kind of religion that would serve their interests, that would serve to perpetuate the existence of slavery. Christianity was used for the purpose of brainwashing, indoctrinating, pacifying.

In his work *The Peculiar Institution*, Kenneth Stampp discusses extensively the role of religion in creating methods of appeasing Black people, of suppressing potential revolt. At first, Africans were not converted to Christianity, because this may have given slaves a claim to freedom. However, the various slave-holding colonies passed laws to the effect that

Black Christians would not automatically become free men by virtue of their baptism. Stampp formulates the reasons why it was finally decided to let slaves through the secret door of Christianity:

> Through religious instruction, the bondman learned that slavery had divine sanction, that insolence was as much an offense against God as against the temporal master. They received the biblical command that servants should obey their masters and they heard of the punishments awaiting the disobedient slave in the hereafter. They heard, too, that eternal salvation would be their reward for faithful service and that on the day of judgment God would deal impartially with the poor and the rich, the black man and white.

Thus those passages in the Bible that emphasized obedience, humility, pacifism, patience, were presented to the slave as the essence of Christianity. Those passages, on the other hand, that talked about equality, freedom, the ones Frederick Douglass was able to discover, because, unlike most slaves, he taught himself to read—these were eliminated from the sermons the slave heard. A very censored version of Christianity was developed especially for the slaves. A pious slave therefore would never hit a white man, his master was always right, even when he was by all human standards wrong. This use of religion was one of the most violent acts against humanity. It was used to teach a group of people that they were not human beings; it was used in attempt to abolish the last remnant of identity that the slave possessed. But, in the long run, this project was not entirely successful as can be witnessed by Frederick Douglass, Gabriel Prosser, Denmark Vesey, Nat Turner, and countless others who turned Christianity against the missionaries. The Old Testament was particularly helpful for those who planned revolts—Children of Israel were delivered out of bondage in Egypt by God—but they fought, they fought in order to carry out the will of God. Resistance was the lesson learned from the Bible. Christian spirituals created and sung by the masses of slaves were also powerful songs of freedom that demonstrate the extent to which Christianity could be rescued from the ideological context forged by the slaveholders and imbued with a revolutionary content of liberation.

Frederick Douglass's reaction to Nat Turner's revolt is revealing. In his later autobiography, *The Life and Times of Frederick Douglass*, he writes,

> The insurrection of Nat Turner had been quelled, but the alarm and terror which it occasioned had not subsided. The cholera was then on its way to this country, and I remember thinking that God was angry with the white people because of their slaveholding wickedness, and therefore his judgments were abroad in the land. Of course it was impossible for me not to hope much for the abolition movement when I saw it supported by the Almighty and armed with death.

I'd like to end here by pointing to the essence of what I have been trying to get across today. The road towards freedom, the path of liberation is marked by resistance at every crossroad: mental resistance, physical resistance, resistance directed to the concerted attempt to obstruct that path. I think we can learn from the experience of the slave. We have to debunk the myth that Black people were docile and accepting and the extreme myth, which by the way I read in my high school history texts in Birmingham, Alabama, that Black people actually preferred slavery to freedom. If you will begin to get into Frederick Douglass, at the next meeting we can try to continue our investigation into the philosophical themes of Black literature.

Before I continue the discussion of Frederick Douglass, I would like to say a few words about the course in general. Black Studies is a field that has long been neglected in the Universities. We are just beginning to fill that vacuum. And we must be very careful, because we do not want Black History, Black Literature to be relegated to the same stagnant, innocuous, compartmentalized existence as, say, the history of the American Revolution. I could talk about Frederick Douglass as if he had the same relevance as, say, the so-called discovering of America by Columbus. History, Literature should not be pieces in a museum of antiquity, especially when they reveal to us problems that continue to exist today. The reasons underlying the demands for Black Studies programs are many, but the most important one is the necessity to establish a continuum from the past to the present, to discover the genesis of problems that continue to exist today, to discover how our ancestors dealt with them. We can learn from the philosophical as well as concrete experience of the slave. We can learn what methods of coming to grips with oppression were historically successful and what methods were failures. The failures are crucial, because we do not want to be responsible for the repetition of history in its brutality. We learn what the mistakes were in order not to duplicate them.

We ought to approach the content in this course not as frozen facts, as static, as meaningful only in terms of understanding the past. We are talking about philosophical themes, recurring philosophical themes. Philosophy is suppose to perform the task of generalizing aspects of experience, and not just for the sake of formulating generalizations, of discovering formulas, as some of my colleagues in the discipline believe. My idea of philosophy is that if it is not relevant to human problems, if it does not tell us how we can go about eradicating some of the misery in this world, then it is not worth the name of philosophy. I think that Socrates made a very profound statement when he asserted that the raison d'être of philosophy is to teach us proper living. In this day and age "proper living" means liberation from the urgent problems of poverty, economic necessity and indoctrination, mental oppression.

Now—let me continue with the course. At our last meeting, I attempted to use the narrative of Frederick Douglass as the occasion for variations on the salient philosophical themes that we encounter in the existence of the slave. The transformation of the idea of freedom into the struggle for liberation via the concept of resistance; this sequence of interdependent themes—freedom, liberation, resistance— provides the groundwork for the course. Within this structure, we discussed last time the extent to which freedom is possible within the limits of slavery. We determined that the very existence of the slave is a contradiction: he is a man who is not a man, that is, a man who does not possess the essential attribute of humanity: freedom. White, slaveholding society defines him as an object, as an animal, as property. The alienation that is thereby produced as the reality of the slave's existence must surface—it must become conscious, if he is to forge a path towards liberation. He must recognize at first the contradictory nature of his existence, and out of the recognition, rejection emerges. We saw that recognition of alienation becomes a prerequisite of and entails rejection, resistance. Religion can play both a positive and a negative role in that road towards self-knowledge. It can thwart liberation—and this is the express purpose for converting the slave—or it can provide powerful assistance, as was the case in Frederick Douglass's first experience of religion.

I'd like to begin today by continuing that discussion of religion. Now, we will discover that Frederick Douglass's interest in and enthusiasm about religion wanes when he apprehends the hypocrisy that accompanied it in the thoughts and actions of the slaveholder. It is important to recognize that the transition from spiritual elevation to disillusionment is ushered in by an actual physical change in the conditions of Frederick Douglass, slave. During the time he developed fervent inclinations towards Christianity as a result of his learning to read, he lived in relatively comfortable circumstances, that is, if anything can be termed comfortable under slavery. His disenchantment occurs when he is forced to live under conditions of actual starvation—when he is given to Captain Thomas Auld.

A critical experience occurs when he observes his brutal and sadistic slavemaster's conversion to Christianity:

> I indulged a faint hope that his conversion would lead him to emancipate his slaves, and that, if he did not do this, it would, at any rate, make him more kind and humane. I was disappointed in both these respects. It neither made him to be humane to his slaves, nor to emancipate them. If it had any effect on his character, it made him more cruel and hateful in all his ways; for I believe him to have been a much worse man after his conversion than before.[42]

These philosophical inferences from what Douglass took to be the essence of Christianity—the demonstration of Christian thoughts by Christian deeds—are refuted by the master's subsequent conduct. For the oppressed, for the slave, religion serves a quite positive purpose: it is a much needed medicine that helps to allay suffering and at the same time it is an inverted consciousness of the world, projection of real needs and desires into supernatural domain. The slaveholder's experience of religion as it is exemplified in the behavior of Captain Auld has an entirely different texture. Religion, for him, is pure ideology which is totally contradictory to his real, day-to-day behavior. The slaveholder must constantly work to maintain that contradiction; his very existence is based on the rigid separation of his real life from his spiritual life. For, if he takes the precepts of Christianity seriously, if he applies them to his daily life, then he would negate his own existence as an oppressor of humanity. Douglass explains: "Prior to his conversion, [Auld] relied upon his own depravity to shield and sustain him in his savage barbarity; but after his conversion, he found religious sanction and support for his slaveholding cruelty."[43]

At least on an unconscious level, there must be some awareness of these contradictions in the mind of the slaveholder. This is indicated by an actual sharpening of the contradictions by Auld himself. The more intense his religious involvement becomes, the more intense becomes his cruelty towards his slaves. An unrelatedness between his religious life and his real life becomes a predictable discontinuity. His increased practice of religion seems to be both an excuse and an expiation before the fact of his increased perpetration of misery among his slaves. Long and loud prayers and hymns justify long and hard flogging, justify outright starvation of the slaves.

What can we infer from this analysis of the slaveholder's relation to religion? As I stated in the last lecture, Western society, and particularly the era of the rule of the bourgeoisie, has been characterized by the gap between theory and practice, particularly between freedom as it is developed conceptually and the lack of freedom in the real world.

The fact that somewhere in one of the foundational documents of this country, there is the statement that all men are created equal and the fact that social and political inequality have never been eradicated cannot be regarded as unrelated to the relative nonchalance with which Master Auld discusses the gap between his religious ideas and his day-to-day precepts. The slaveholder's own words reveal to us the brutality that underlies not only his particular situation, but that of society in general. We sometimes have to resort to the most extreme examples in order to uncover veiled meanings of the more subtle example.

Frederick Douglass's recognition of the contradictions between religious ideas and the behavior of his master brings him to a critical disposition toward the relevance of religion itself:

> I assert most unhesitatingly, that the religion of the south is a mere covering for the most horrid crimes,—a justifier of the most appalling barbarity,—a sanctifier of the most hateful frauds,—and a dark shelter under which the darkest, foulest, grossest, and most infernal deeds of slaveholders find the strongest protection. Were I to be again reduced to the chains of slavery, next to that enslavement, I should regard being the slave of a religious master the greatest calamity that could befall me.[44]

Last time we pointed to Marx's interpretation of the role that religion plays in the society. I would like to point to some further observations he makes concerning religion in the *Contribution to the Critique of Hegel's Philosophy of Right.* I think that Marx's analysis of religion helps us to understand the state of Frederick Douglass when he begins to turn away from religion. I quote a passage from that work:

> *Religious* suffering is at the same time an expression of real suffering and a *protest* against real suffering. Religion is the sigh of the oppressed creature, the sentiment of a heartless world, and the soul of soulless conditions. It is the opium of the people.
>
> The abolition of religion as the illusory happiness of men, is a demand for their *real* happiness. The call to abandon their illusions about their condition is a *call to abandon a condition which requires illusions.*

Frederick Douglass existentially experiences what Marx theoretically formulates. He sees through the veil of illusion in observing the rather schizophrenic behavior of his master relative to his religion and his daily life. It is not insignificant that this enlightenment emerges, as I have indicated before, at a time when his physical suffering becomes practically unbearable. We can infer that in seeing through the hypocrisy of his master, he attains a certain self-consciousness, self-knowledge. The master becomes a mirror of his own past escape. Situated in relative comfort, he had the luxury to think in metaphysical categories. Now he must come face to face with the absolute necessity to eradicate, to destroy his suffering. "Religion, Marx says, is only the illusory sun about which man revolves so long as he does not revolve about himself."

Frederick Douglass gathers the courage to resist the slave-breaker to whom he is sent for domestication, for taming—the slave-breaker who is infinitely more brutal than any of his previous masters. He finds this courage when he is able to free himself of his religion. "I love the pure, peaceable, and impartial Christianity of Christ: I therefore hate the corrupt, slaveholding, women-whipping, cradle-plundering, partial and hypocritical Christianity of this land. Indeed, I can see no reason, but the most deceitful one, for calling the religion of this land Christianity."[10]

So we find that the role of religion during the era of slavery is not homogenous: it is extremely complex. The function of religion continually reverts from one extreme to the other. No one formula can suffice. If we saw at the last meeting that religion can play a positive role, now we are uncovering the detrimental aspects, how it suppressed the slave in the person of the slaveholder, how it provided internal control and thus how it must often be transcended in order for real change to take place. Religious leaders of slave revolts found inspiration in religion, they found courage in it. Frederick Douglass, at this point in his life, as well as countless other people, saw the necessity to cancel out illusions in order to transform the real world, in order to arrive at a total commitment to resist oppression.

I concur with Marx that one must overcome religion in

order to regain one's reason, that the sigh of the oppressed creature in order to become an effective protest against oppression, must be articulated and acted upon in a political context. Yet, I do not deny that to a certain extent, the illusory nature of religion may well be transcended within the limits of religion—I gave Nat Turner, Denmark Vesey, Gabriel Prosser as examples last time. By the way, someone brought to my attention that I did not mention any women among these examples. I was not on my toes. The accomplishments of Harriet Tubman, Sojourner Truth, and many others can never be overestimated.

I would like to leave the discussion of religion now—perhaps we will take it up again at a further point in the life of Frederick Douglass. I would like to continue to develop the notion of alienation and how the slave experiences the world and history. We said that the extreme formulation of the slave's alienation is his existence as property, as capital, as money. There is a relatively long quotation from Douglass's later work, *The Life and Times of Frederick Douglass*, that I would like to take the time to read, because I feel it epitomizes by its very concreteness the notion of alienation.

> I am, thought I, but the sport of a power which makes no account either of my welfare or of my happiness. By a law which I can comprehend, but cannot evade or resist, I am ruthlessly snatched away from the hearth of a fond grandmother and hurried away to the home of a mysterious old master; again I am removed from there to a

master in Baltimore; thence am I snatched away to the
Eastern Shore to be valued with the beasts of the field,
and with them divided and set apart for a possessor;
then I am sent back to Baltimore, and by the time I have
formed new attachments and have begun to hope that
no more rude shocks shall touch me, a difference arises
between brothers, and I am again broken up and sent to
St. Michaels; and now from the latter place I am foot-
ing my way to the home of another master, where, I am
given to understand, like a wild young working animal
I am to be broken to the yoke of a bitter and lifelong
bondage.

For the slave, the world appears as a hostile network of
circumstances that continually are to his disadvantage. History is experienced as a cluster of chance events, accidental
occurrences which, though far beyond his control, act in a
way that is usually detrimental to his personal life. A trivial
quarrel between brothers is enough to wreak and mutilate
the slave's life—Frederick Douglass is brought back to the
plantation of his real owner, one who is infinitely more sadistic than the brother with whom he had been living, as a
result of such a banal disagreement.

Yesterday one of the white students in the class came to
my office and wanted to know how I was going to conduct
the course. He asked whether or not I was going to limit the
course to the philosophical experiences of the slave, of the
Black man in society, or whether I was going to talk about

people. Now, aside from the fact that slaves and Black people are people, there is something in my mind that I think you should be aware of—and it is not unrelated to what I was just saying about alienation. Oppressed people are forced to come to grips with immediate problems every day, problems that have a philosophical status and are relevant to all people. One such problem is that of alienation. It is my opinion that most people living in Western society today are alienated, alienated from themselves, from society. To provide an objective demonstration of this would require some discussion, and if you like, we can take this up in one of the discussion periods. The point is that the slave, the Black man, the Chicano and oppressed whites are much more aware of alienation, perhaps not as a philosophical concept, but as a fact of their daily existence. The slave, for example, experiences that alienation as the continual hostility of all his daily surroundings. During the era of slavery, I suppose it was common opinion that the slave was in bondage and the white man was free, the Black man was non- or subhuman and the white man was the apex of humanity. Again, let us take a look at the extreme example of the white man in slaveholding society—the slave-breaker. There is something that I think we might call the concept of the slave-breaker and we can unfold this concept according to the concrete behavior of Covey, the Negro-breaker under whose authority Frederick Douglass lives for a year.

Now, what do we mean by the concept of the slave-breaker? His existence is the *sine qua non* of slavery, an indispensable fact for the perpetuation of slavery. At the same time, the slave-breaker finds himself almost on the margin of slavery, the last barrier between physical enslavement and physical liberation. He is the one designated to tame impudent slaves, slaves who refuse to accept for themselves the definition that society has imposed upon them. He must break, destroy the human being in the slave before it succeeds in upsetting the whole balance present in the system of slavery. His instrument is violence. He does violence to the body in order to break the will. Not only continual whipping, but work, labor not fit for a beast of burden were the manifestations of that violence.

> Just as I got into the woods, he came up and told me to stop my cart, and that he would teach me how to trifle away my time, and break gates. He then went to a large gum-tree, and with his axe cut three large switches, and, after trimming them up neatly with his pocket-knife, he ordered me to take off my clothes. I made him no answer, but stood with my clothes on. He repeated his order. I still made him no answer, nor did I move to strip myself. Upon this he rushed at me with the fierceness of a tiger, tore off my clothes, and lashed me till he had worn out his switches, cutting me so savagely as to leave the marks visible for a long time after. This whipping was the first of a number just like it, and for similar offences.
>
> I lived with Mr. Covey one year. During that first six

months, of that year, scarce a week passed without his whipping me. I was seldom free from a sore back. My awkwardness was almost always his excuse for whipping me. We were worked fully up to the point of endurance. Long before day we were up, our horses fed, and by the first approach of day we were off to the field with our hoes and ploughing teams. Mr. Covey gave us enough to eat, but scarce time to eat it. We were often less than five minutes taking our meals. We were often in the field from the first approach of day till its last lingering ray had left us; and at saving-fodder time, midnight often caught us in the field binding blades.[45]

One of the lessons we can learn from the dialectical method is that in the process of functioning in the world, man undergoes changes himself that are consonant with his actions. That is, man cannot perform a task in the world without himself being affected by that performance. Now, what does this mean for Covey, the Negro-breaker? His task is to mutilate the humanity of the slave. The question we must ask ourselves is whether he can perform that task without mutilating his own humanity. We ought to be able to infer, from the answer to this question, what happened to the humanity of the white man in general during the era of slavery.

We don't have to engage in any unnecessary philosophizing in order to answer that question. Frederick Douglass says it outright, he calls the slave-breaker by his name.

There was no deceiving him. His work went on in his absence almost as well as in his presence; and he had the faculty of making us feel that he was ever present with us. This he did by surprising us. He seldom approached the spot where we were at work openly, if he could do it secretly. He always aimed at taking us by surprise. Such was his cunning, that we used to call him, among ourselves, "the snake." When we were at work in the cornfield, he would sometimes crawl on has hands and knees to avoid detection, and all at once he would rise nearly in our midst, and scream out. . . . His comings were like a thief in the night. He appeared to us as being ever at hand. He was under every tree, behind every stump, in every bush, and at every window, on the plantation.[46]

Who is the non-human here? Who lowers himself to the depths? Aside from the Biblical imagery of the serpent as the representative of evil, the image of the snake, his very posture, crawling around on the ground, is symbolic and revealing. In order to induce the slaves to labor, the slave-breaker lies, he is forced to lie, he is inhuman and is forced to be inhuman. He takes on the characteristics of the very task he sees himself as performing. I would go so far as to say that he is even more profoundly affected than the slave, for the slave can see what is occurring— he is aware of the fact that there is an external power dedicated to the suppression of the slave's basic human existence. He sees it, feels it, hears it in every act of the slave-breaker.

The slave-breaker on the other hand is unaware of the change he himself is undergoing as a result of his sadistic actions:

> Mr. Covey's *forte* consisted in his power to deceive. His life was devoted to planning and perpetrating the grossest deceptions. Every thing he possessed in the shape of learning or religion, he made conform to his disposition to deceive. He seemed to think himself equal to deceive the Almighty.[47]

This tendency towards unconscious self-annihilation was not confined to the slave-breaker, to those who stood at the boundaries of slavery in order to maintain those boundaries. These characteristics were direct results of the system itself and could be attributed to slaveholders in general. As Douglass would later write, "Mean and contemptible as all this is, it is in keeping with the character which the life of a slaveholder was calculated to produce."[48]

And in referring to the naturalness of Mr. Covey's trickery and inclination to lie, Frederick Douglass later wrote, "It was an important system essential to the relation of master and slave."[49]

Let's continue to discuss this relation of master and slave and its effects on the master. As we were saying, the master is thought to be free, independent; the slave is thought to be unfree, dependent. The freedom and independence of the master, if we look at it philosophically, is a myth. It is one of those myths which, I was saying at the last session, we have to uncover in order to reach the real substance behind it. How could the master have been independent when it is the very institution of slavery that provided his wealth, that provided his means of sustenance? The master was dependent on the slave, dependent for his life on the slave.

In the *Phenomenology of Mind*, Hegel discusses the dialectical relationship between the slave and the master. He states, among other things, that the master, in reaching a consciousness of his own condition, must become aware that his very independence is based on his dependence on the slave. This might sound a bit contradictory, but then dialectics is based on discovering the contradictions in phenomena which can alone account for their existence. Reality is permeated through and through with contradictions. Without those contradictions, there would be no movement, no process, no activity. I don't want to go off on a theoretical tangent about dialectics, so let us get back to the slave and the master and see the dialectical relationship as it is actually practiced in reality. The independence of the master, we were saying, is based on his dependence on the slave. If the slave were not there to till the land, to build his estates, to serve him his meals, the master would not be free from the necessities of life. If he had to do all the things that the slave does for him, he would be just as much in a state of bondage as the slave. Only, the slave is the buffer-zone, and in this sense, the slave is somewhat of a master—it is the slave who possesses the power over the life of the master: if he does not work, when he ceases to follow orders, the master's means of sustaining himself has disappeared.

So, at this point we can make the following statement—and I hope it is clear. The master is always on the verge of becoming the slave and the slave possesses the real, concrete power to make him always on the verge of becoming the master.

I don't want this to sound like a whole lot of philosophical word games. Sometimes, when one reads Hegel, one has the impression that this is what he is doing—playing with our minds: things are themselves, but they are constantly becoming other than themselves, they are constantly becoming their own contradictions.

I think I can demonstrate the truth of the proposition that the master is always on the verge of becoming the slave and the slave is always on the verge of becoming the master. Let's look at what I think is the most crucial passage in the *Narrative of the Life of Frederick Douglass*. It can be found in Chapter X. Frederick Douglass has just had the harrowing experience of being driven to work until the point when he physically collapses. At this point he has been broken—mentally his will is gone. Covey, refusing to accept his illness as a valid excuse for failure to continue, beats him while he is lying on the ground unable to move. Frederick Douglass decides to return to his master, but, finding no form of compassion in the reaction of his master, returns. Fortunately, it is on a Sunday when he finally reaches the slave-breaker's house and because of his devoutness, Mr. Covey does not beat him—or, as Sandy, a slave who has helped Frederick Douglass would like us to believe, Mr. Covey does not beat him as a result of the magical powers of a root that he has given to him. At any rate, the slave-breaker does not enter into the person of Mr. Covey until after the Sabbath is over. Instinctively, unconsciously, Frederick Douglass fights back when the slave-breaker attempts to beat him:

> Mr. Covey seemed now to think he had me, and could do what he pleased; but at this moment—from whence came the spirit I don't know—I resolved to fight; and, suiting my action to the resolution, I seized Covey hard by the throat; and as I did so, I rose.[50]

What is the reaction of Mr. Covey? One would think that because, after all he is the master, he is white, he would have no problems conquering a sixteen-year-old boy. The slave-breaker, who has the reputation of being able to tame the wild-animal slaves from all around, trembles and calls for help: "Covey at length let me go, puffing and blowing at a great rate, saying that if I had not resisted, he would not have whipped me half so much. The truth was, that he had not whipped me at all."[51] He unsuccessfully calls upon a slave who is not under his authority, for aid. He eventually attempts to command his own slave, a woman, to conquer Frederick. She refuses, and he is left helpless.

We have to ask ourselves what is happening here. Covey is certainly physically strong enough to overpower Frederick. Why is he unable to cope with that unexpected resistance? That act of open resistance challenges his very identity. He is no longer the recognized master, the slave no longer recognizes himself as slave. The roles have been reversed. And think about this as a concrete example of that proposition I put forth earlier—that the master is always on the verge of becoming the slave and the slave is always on the verge of becoming the master. Here, it has happened. Covey implicitly recognizes the fact that he is dependent on the slave, not only in a material sense, not only for the production of wealth, but also for the affirmation of his own identity. The fact that he appeals to all the slaves around him to help him overpower Frederick indicates that he is dependent on that affirmation of his authority—they all reject it, and he is left in a vacuum—alienated from himself. This has the effect of sapping whatever physical strength he may have needed in order to win the battle.

After having obviously lost the battle, with no substantial basis for his own identity, his own role, he nonetheless attempts to reassert his authority:

> Covey at length let me go, puffing and blowing at a great
> rate, saying that if I had not resisted, he would not have

whipped me half so much. The truth was, that he had not whipped me at all. I considered him as getting entirely the worst end of the bargain; for he had drawn no blood from me, but I had from him.[52]

Covey never again attempted to whip him. Frederick Douglass describes this incident as the turning point in his life as a slave

NARRATIVE

OF THE

LIFE

OF

FREDERICK DOUGLASS,

AN

AMERICAN SLAVE

WRITTEN BY HIMSELF

Frederick Douglass

In the month of August, 1841, I attended an anti-slavery convention in Nantucket, at which it was my happiness to become acquainted with FREDERICK DOUGLASS, the writer of the following Narrative. He was a stranger to nearly every member of that body; but, having recently made his escape from the southern prison-house of bondage, and feeling his curiosity excited to ascertain the principles and measures of the abolitionists,—of whom he had heard a somewhat vague description while he was a slave,—he was induced to give his attendance, on the occasion alluded to, though at that time a resident in New Bedford.

Fortunate, most fortunate occurrence!—fortunate for the millions of his manacled brethren, yet panting for deliverance from their awful thraldom!—fortunate for the cause of negro emancipation, and of universal liberty!—fortunate for the land of his birth, which he has already done so much to save and bless!—fortunate for a large circle of friends and acquaintances, whose sympathy and affection he has strongly secured by the many sufferings he has endured, by his virtuous traits of character, by his ever-abiding remembrance of those who are in bonds, as being bound with them!—fortunate for the multitudes, in various parts of our republic, whose minds he has enlightened on the subject of slavery, and who have been melted to tears by his pathos, or roused to virtuous indignation by his stirring eloquence against the enslavers of men!—fortunate for himself, as it at once brought him into the field of public usefulness, "gave the world assurance of a MAN," quickened the slumbering energies of his soul, and consecrated him to the great work of breaking the rod of the oppressor, and letting the oppressed go free!

I shall never forget his first speech at the convention—the extraordinary emotion it excited in my own mind—the powerful impression it created upon a crowded auditory, completely taken by surprise—the applause which followed from the beginning to the end of his felicitous remarks. I think I never hated slavery so intensely as at that moment; certainly, my perception of the enormous outrage which is inflicted by it, on the godlike nature of its victims, was rendered far more clear than ever. There stood one, in physical proportion and stature commanding and exact—in intellect richly endowed—in natural eloquence a prodigy—in soul manifestly "created but a little lower than the angels"—yet a slave, ay, a fugitive slave,—trembling for his safety, hardly daring to believe that on the American soil, a single white person could be found who would befriend him at all hazards, for the love of God and humanity! Capable of high attainments as an intellectual and moral being—needing nothing but a comparatively small amount of cultivation to make him an ornament to society and a blessing to his race—by the law of the land, by the voice of the people, by the terms of the slave code, he was only a piece of property, a beast of burden, a chattel personal, nevertheless!

A beloved friend from New Bedford prevailed on MR. DOUGLASS to address the convention. He came forward to the platform with a hesitancy and embarrassment, necessarily the attendants of a sensitive mind in such a novel position. After apologizing for his ignorance, and reminding the audience that slavery was a poor school for the human intellect and heart, he proceeded to narrate some of the facts in his own history as a slave, and in the course of his speech gave utterance to many noble thoughts and thrilling reflections. As soon as he had taken his seat, filled with hope and admiration, I rose, and declared that PATRICK HENRY, of revolutionary fame, never made a speech more eloquent in the cause of liberty, than the one we had just listened to from the lips of that hunted fugitive. So I believed at that time,—such is my belief now. I reminded the audience of the peril which surrounded this self-emancipated young man at the North,—even in Massachusetts, on the soil of the Pilgrim Fathers, among the descendants of revolutionary sires; and I appealed to them, whether they would ever allow him to be carried back into slavery,—law or no law, constitution or no constitution. The response was unanimous and in thunder-tones—"NO!" "Will you succor and protect him as a brother-man—a resident of the old Bay State?" "YES!" shouted the whole mass, with an energy so startling, that the ruthless tyrants south of Mason and Dixon's line might almost have heard the mighty burst of feeling, and recognized it as the pledge of an invincible determination, on the part of those who gave it, never to betray him that wanders, but to hide the outcast, and firmly to abide the consequences.

It was at once deeply impressed upon my mind, that, if MR. DOUGLASS could be persuaded to consecrate his time and talents to the promotion of the anti-slavery enterprise, a powerful impetus would be given to it, and a stunning blow at the same time inflicted on northern prejudice against a colored complexion. I therefore endeavored to instil hope and courage into his mind, in order that he might dare to engage in a vocation so anomalous and responsible for a person in his situation; and I was seconded in this effort by warm-hearted friends, especially by the late General Agent of the Massachusetts Anti-Slavery Society, MR. JOHN A. COLLINS, whose judgment in this instance entirely coincided with my own. At first, he could give no encouragement; with unfeigned diffidence, he expressed his conviction that he was not adequate to the performance of so great a task; the path marked out was wholly an untrodden one; he was sincerely apprehensive that he should do more harm than good. After much deliberation, however, he consented to make a trial; and ever since that period, he has acted as a lecturing agent, under the auspices either of the American or the Massachusetts Anti-Slavery Society. In labors he has been most abundant; and his success in combating prejudice, in gaining proselytes, in agitating the public mind, has far surpassed the most sanguine expectations that were raised at the commencement of his brilliant career. He has borne himself with gentleness and meekness, yet with true manliness of character. As a public speaker, he excels in pathos, wit, comparison, imitation, strength of reasoning, and fluency of language. There is in him that union of head and heart, which is indispensable to an enlightenment of the heads and a winning of the hearts of others. May his strength continue to be equal to his day! May he continue to "grow in grace, and in the knowledge of God," that he may be increasingly serviceable in the cause of bleeding humanity, whether at home or abroad!

It is certainly a very remarkable fact, that one of the most efficient advocates of the slave population, now before the public, is a fugitive slave, in the person of FREDERICK DOUGLASS; and that the free colored population of the United States are as ably represented by one of their own number, in the person of CHARLES LENOX REMOND, whose eloquent appeals have extorted the highest applause of multitudes on both sides of the Atlantic. Let the calumniators of the colored race despise themselves for their baseness and illiberality of spirit, and henceforth cease to talk of the natural inferiority of those who require nothing but time and opportunity to attain to the highest point of human excellence.

It may, perhaps, be fairly questioned, whether any other portion of the population of the earth could have endured the privations, sufferings and horrors of slavery, without having become more degraded in the scale of humanity than the slaves of African descent. Nothing has been left undone to cripple their intellects, darken their minds, debase their moral nature, obliterate all traces of their relationship to mankind; and yet how wonderfully they have sustained the mighty load of a most frightful bondage, under which they have been groaning for centuries! To illustrate the effect of slavery on the white man,—to show that he has no powers of endurance, in such a condition, superior to those of his black brother,—DANIEL O'CONNELL, the distinguished advocate of universal emancipation, and the mightiest champion of prostrate but not conquered Ireland, relates the following anecdote in a speech delivered by him in the Conciliation Hall, Dublin, before the Loyal National Repeal Association, March 31, 1845. "No matter," said MR. O'CONNELL, "under what specious term it may disguise itself, slavery is still hideous. *It has a natural, an inevitable tendency to brutalize every noble faculty of man.* An American sailor, who was cast away on the shore of Africa, where he was kept in slavery for three years, was, at the expiration of that period, found to be imbruted and stultified—he had lost all reasoning power; and having forgotten his native language, could only utter some savage gibberish between Arabic and English, which nobody could understand, and which even he himself found difficulty in pronouncing. So much for the humanizing influence of THE DOMESTIC INSTITUTION!" Admitting this to have been an extraordinary case of mental deterioration, it proves at least that the white slave can sink as low in the scale of humanity as the black one.

Mr. DOUGLASS has very properly chosen to write his own Narrative, in his own style, and according to the best of his ability, rather than to employ some one else. It is, therefore, entirely his own production; and, considering how long and dark was the career he had to run as a slave,—how few have been his opportunities to improve his mind since he broke his iron fetters—it is, in my judgment, highly creditable to his head and heart. He who can peruse it without a tearful eye, a heaving breast, an afflicted spirit,—without being filled with an unutterable abhorrence of slavery and all its abettors, and animated with a determination to seek the immediate overthrow of that execrable system,—without trembling for the fate of this country in the hands of a righteous God, who is ever on the side of the oppressed, and whose arm is not shortened that it cannot save,—must have a flinty heart, and be qualified to act the part of a trafficker "in slaves and the souls of men." I am confident that it is essentially true in all its statements; that nothing has been set down in malice, nothing exaggerated, nothing drawn from the imagination; that it comes short of the reality, rather than overstates a single fact in regard to SLAVERY AS IT IS. The experience of FREDERICK DOUGLASS, as a slave, was not a peculiar one; his lot was not especially a hard one; his case may be regarded as a very fair specimen of the treatment of slaves in Maryland, in which State it is conceded that they are better fed and less cruelly treated than in Georgia, Alabama, or Louisiana. Many have suffered incomparably more, while very few on the plantations have suffered less, than himself. Yet how deplorable was his situation! what terrible chastisements were inflicted upon his person! what still more shocking outrages were perpetrated upon his mind! with all his noble powers and sublime aspirations, how like a brute was he treated, even by those professing to have the same mind in them that was in Christ Jesus! to what dreadful liabilities was he continually subjected! how destitute of friendly counsel and aid, even in his greatest extremities! how heavy was the midnight of woe which shrouded in blackness the last ray of hope, and filled the future with terror and gloom! what longings after freedom took possession of his breast, and how his misery augmented, in proportion as he grew reflective and intelligent,—thus demonstrating that a happy slave is an extinct man! how he thought, reasoned, felt, under the lash of the driver, with the chains upon his limbs! what perils he encountered in his endeavors to escape from his horrible doom! and how signal have been his deliverance and preservation in the midst of a nation of pitiless enemies!

This Narrative contains many affecting incidents, many passages of great eloquence and power; but I think the most thrilling one of them all is the description DOUGLASS gives of his feelings, as he stood soliloquizing respecting his fate, and the chances of his one day being a freeman, on the banks of the Chesapeake Bay—viewing the receding vessels as they flew with their white wings before the breeze, and apostrophizing them as animated by the living spirit of freedom. Who can read that passage, and be insensible to its pathos and sublimity? Compressed into it is a whole Alexandrian library of thought, feeling, and sentiment—all that can, all that need be urged, in the form of expostulation, entreaty, rebuke, against that crime of crimes,—making man the property of his fellow-man! O, how accursed is that system, which entombs the godlike mind of man, defaces the divine image, reduces those who by creation were crowned with glory and honor to a level with four-footed beasts, and exalts the dealer in human flesh above all that is called God! Why should its existence be prolonged one hour? Is it not evil, only evil, and that continually? What does its presence imply but the absence of all fear of God, all regard for man, on the part of the people of the United States? Heaven speed its eternal overthrow!

So profoundly ignorant of the nature of slavery are many persons, that they are stubbornly incredulous whenever they read or listen to any recital of the cruelties which are daily inflicted on its victims. They do not deny that the slaves are held as property; but that terrible fact seems to convey to their minds no idea of injustice, exposure to outrage, or savage barbarity. Tell them of cruel scourgings, of mutilations and brandings, of scenes of pollution and blood, of the banishment of all light and knowledge, and they affect to be greatly indignant at such enormous exaggerations, such wholesale misstatements, such abominable libels on the character of the southern planters! As if all these direful outrages were not the natural results of slavery! As if it were less cruel to reduce a human being to the condition of a thing, than to give him a severe flagellation, or to deprive him of necessary food and clothing! As if whips, chains, thumbscrews, paddles, bloodhounds, overseers, drivers, patrols, were not all indispensable to keep the slaves down, and to give protection to their ruthless oppressors! As if, when the marriage institution is abolished, concubinage, adultery, and incest, must not necessarily abound; when all the rights of humanity are annihilated, any barrier remains to protect the victim from the fury of the spoiler; when absolute power is assumed over life and liberty, it will not be wielded with destructive sway! Skeptics of this character abound in society. In some few instances, their incredulity arises from a want of reflection; but, generally, it indicates a hatred of the light, a desire to shield slavery from the assaults of its foes, a contempt of the colored race, whether bond or free. Such will try to discredit the shocking tales of slaveholding cruelty which are recorded in this truthful Narrative; but they will labor in vain. MR. DOUGLASS has frankly disclosed the place of his birth, the names of those who claimed ownership in his body and soul, and the names also of those who committed the crimes which he has alleged against them. His statements, therefore, may easily be disproved, if they are untrue.

In the course of his Narrative, he relates two instances of murderous cruelty,—in one of which a planter deliberately shot a slave belonging to a neighboring plantation, who had unintentionally gotten within his lordly domain in quest of fish; and in the other, an overseer blew out the brains of a slave who had fled to a stream of water to escape a bloody scourging. MR. DOUGLASS states that in neither of these instances was any thing done by way of legal arrest or judicial investigation. The Baltimore American, of March 17, 1845, relates a similar case of atrocity, perpetrated with similar impunity—as follows:—"*Shooting a Slave.*—We learn, upon the authority of a letter from Charles county, Maryland, received by a gentleman of this city, that a young man, named Matthews, a nephew of General Matthews, and whose father, it is believed, holds an office at Washington, killed one of the slaves upon his father's farm by shooting him. The letter states that young Matthews had been left in charge of the farm; that he gave an order to the servant, which was disobeyed, when he proceeded to the house, *obtained a gun, and, returning, shot the servant.* He immediately, the letter continues, fled to his father's residence, where he still remains unmolested."—Let it never be forgotten, that no slaveholder or overseer can be convicted of any outrage perpetrated on the person of a slave, however diabolical it may be, on the testimony of colored witnesses, whether bond or free. By the slave code, they are adjudged to be as incompetent to testify against a white man, as though they were indeed a part of the brute creation. Hence, there is no legal protection in fact, whatever there may be in form, for the slave population; and any amount of cruelty may be inflicted on them with impunity. Is it possible for the human mind to conceive of a more horrible state of society?

The effect of a religious profession on the conduct of southern masters is vividly described in the following Narrative, and shown to be any thing but salutary. In the nature of the case, it must be in the highest degree pernicious. The testimony of Mr. Douglass, on this point, is sustained by a cloud of witnesses, whose veracity is unimpeachable. "A slaveholder's profession of Christianity is a palpable imposture. He is a felon of the highest grade. He is a man-stealer. It is of no importance what you put in the other scale."

Reader! are you with the man-stealers in sympathy and purpose, or on the side of their down-trodden victims? If with the former, then are you the foe of God and man. If with the latter, what are you prepared to do and dare in their behalf? Be faithful, be vigilant, be untiring in your efforts to break every yoke, and let the oppressed go free. Come what may—cost what it may—inscribe on the banner which you unfurl to the breeze, as your religious and political motto—"No Compromise with Slavery! No Union with Slaveholders!"

WM. LLOYD GARRISON.

Boston, *May* 1, 1845.

LETTER

From Wendell Phillips, Esq.

Boston, *April 22, 1845.*

My Dear Friend:

You remember the old fable of "The Man and the Lion,"
where the lion complained that he should not be so misrep-
resented "when the lions write history."

I am glad the time has come when the "lions write history." We have been left long enough to gather the character of slavery from the involuntary evidence of the masters.
One might, indeed, rest sufficiently satisfied with what, it is
evident, must be, in general the results of such a relation,
without seeking farther to find whether they have followed
in every instance. Indeed, those who stare at the half-peck
of corn a week, and love to count the lashes on the slave's
back, are seldom the "stuff" out of which reformers and
abolitionists are to be made. I remember that, in 1838, many
were waiting for the results of the West India experiment,
before they could come into our ranks. Those "results" have
come long ago; but, alas! few of that number have come
with them, as converts. A man must be disposed to judge of
emancipation by other tests than whether it has increased

the produce of sugar,—and to hate slavery for other reasons than because it starves men and whips women,—before he is ready to lay the first stone of his anti-slavery life.

I was glad to learn, in your story, how early the most neglected of God's children waken to a sense of their rights, and of the injustice done them. Experience is a keen teacher; and long before you had mastered your A B C, or knew where the "white sails" of the Chesapeake were bound, you began, I see, to gauge the wretchedness of the slave, not by his hunger and want, not by his lashes and toil, but by the cruel and blighting death which gathers over his soul.

In connection with this, there is one circumstance which makes your recollections peculiarly valuable, and renders your early insight the more remarkable. You come from that part of the country where we are told slavery appears with its fairest features. Let us hear, then, what it is at its best estate—gaze on its bright side, if it has one; and then imagination may task her powers to add dark lines to the picture, as she travels southward to that (for the colored man) Valley of the Shadow of Death, where the Mississippi sweeps along.

Again, we have known you long, and can put the most entire confidence in your truth, candor, and sincerity. Every one who has heard you speak has felt, and, I am confident, every one who reads your book will feel, persuaded that you give them a fair specimen of the whole truth. No one-sided portrait,—no wholesale complaints,—but strict justice done, whenever individual kindliness has neutralized, for a moment, the deadly system with which it was strangely allied. You have been with us, too, some years, and can fairly compare the twilight of rights, which your race enjoy at the North, with that "noon of night" under which they labor south of Mason and Dixon's line. Tell us whether, after all, the half-free colored man of Massachusetts is worse off than the pampered slave of the rice swamps!

In reading your life, no one can say that we have unfairly picked out some rare specimens of cruelty. We know that the bitter drops, which even you have drained from the cup, are no incidental aggravations, no individual ills, but such as must mingle always and necessarily in the lot of every slave. They are the essential ingredients, not the occasional results, of the system.

After all, I shall read your book with trembling for you. Some years ago, when you were beginning to tell me your real name and birthplace, you may remember I stopped you, and preferred to remain ignorant of all. With the exception of a vague description, so I continued, till the other day, when you read me your memoirs. I hardly knew, at the time, whether to thank you or not for the sight of them, when I reflected that it was still dangerous, in Massachusetts, for honest men to tell their names! They say the fathers, in 1776, signed the Declaration of Independence with the halter about their necks. You, too, publish your declaration of freedom with danger compassing you around. In all the broad lands which the Constitution of the United States overshadows, there is no single spot,—however narrow or desolate,—where a fugitive slave can plant himself and say, "I am safe." The whole armory of Northern Law has no shield for you. I am free to say that, in your place, I should throw the MS. into the fire.

You, perhaps, may tell your story in safety, endeared as you are to so many warm hearts by rare gifts, and a still rarer devotion of them to the service of others. But it will be owing only to your labors, and the fearless efforts of those who, trampling the laws and Constitution of the country under their feet, are determined that they will "hide the outcast," and that their hearths shall be, spite of the law, an asylum for the oppressed, if, some time or other, the humblest may stand in our streets, and bear witness in safety against the cruelties of which he has been the victim.

Yet it is sad to think, that these very throbbing hearts which welcome your story, and form your best safeguard in telling it, are all beating contrary to the "statute in such case made and provided." Go on, my dear friend, till you, and those who, like you, have been saved, so as by fire, from the dark prison-house, shall stereotype these free, illegal pulses into statutes; and New England, cutting loose from a blood-stained Union, shall glory in being the house of refuge for the oppressed;—till we no longer merely "hide the outcast," or make a merit of standing idly by while he is hunted in our midst; but, consecrating anew the soil of the Pilgrims as an asylum for the oppressed, proclaim our *welcome* to the slave so loudly, that the tones shall reach every hut in the Carolinas, and make the broken-hearted bondman leap up at the thought of old Massachusetts.

God speed the day!

Till then, and ever,
Yours truly,
WENDELL PHILLIPS.

FREDERICK DOUGLASS.

NARRATIVE OF THE LIFE OF

FREDERICK DOUGLASS

CHAPTER I

I was born in Tuckahoe, near Hillsborough, and about twelve miles from Easton, in Talbot county, Maryland. I have no accurate knowledge of my age, never having seen any authentic record containing it. By far the larger part of the slaves know as little of their ages as horses know of theirs, and it is the wish of most masters within my knowledge to keep their slaves thus ignorant. I do not remember to have ever met a slave who could tell of his birthday. They seldom come nearer to it than planting-time, harvest-time, cherry-time, spring-time, or fall-time. A want of information concerning my own was a source of unhappiness to me even during childhood. The white children could tell their ages. I could not tell why I ought to be deprived of the same privilege. I was not allowed to make any inquiries of my master concerning it. He deemed all such inquiries on the part of a slave improper and impertinent, and evidence of a restless spirit. The nearest estimate I can give makes me now between twenty-seven and twenty-eight years of age. I come to this, from hearing my master say, some time during 1835, I was about seventeen years old.

My mother was named Harriet Bailey. She was the daughter of Isaac and Betsey Bailey, both colored, and quite dark. My mother was of a darker complexion than either my grandmother or grandfather.

My father was a white man. He was admitted to be such by all I ever heard speak of my parentage. The opinion was also whispered that my master was my father; but of the correctness of this opinion, I know nothing; the means of knowing was withheld from me. My mother and I were separated when I was but an infant—before I knew her as my mother. It is a common custom, in the part of Maryland from which I ran away, to part children from their mothers at a very early age. Frequently, before the child has reached its twelfth month, its mother is taken from it, and hired out on some farm a considerable distance off, and the child is placed under the care of an old woman, too old for field labor. For what this separation is done, I do not know, unless it be to hinder the development of the child's affection toward its mother, and to blunt and destroy the natural affection of the mother for the child. This is the inevitable result.

I never saw my mother, to know her as such, more than four or five times in my life; and each of these times was very short in duration, and at night. She was hired by a Mr. Stewart, who lived about twelve miles from my home. She made her journeys to see me in the night, travelling the whole distance on foot, after the performance of her day's work. She was a field hand, and a whipping is the penalty of not being in the field at sunrise, unless a slave has special permission from his or her master to the contrary—a permission which they seldom get, and one that gives to him that gives it the proud name of being a kind master. I do not recollect of ever seeing my mother by the light of day. She was with me in the night. She would lie down with me, and get me to sleep, but long before I waked she was gone. Very little communication ever took place between us. Death soon ended what little we could have while she lived, and with it her hardships and suffering. She died when I was about seven years old, on one of my master's farms, near Lee's Mill. I was not allowed to be present during her illness, at her death, or burial. She was gone long before I knew any thing about it. Never having enjoyed, to any considerable extent, her soothing presence, her tender and watchful care, I received the tidings of her death with much the same emotions I should have probably felt at the death of a stranger.

Called thus suddenly away, she left me without the slightest intimation of who my father was. The whisper that my master was my father, may or may not be true; and, true or false, it is of but little consequence to my purpose whilst the fact remains, in all its glaring odiousness, that slaveholders have ordained, and by law established, that the children of slave women shall in all cases follow the condition of their mothers; and this is done too obviously to administer to their own lusts, and make a gratification of their wicked desires profitable as well as pleasurable; for by this cunning arrangement, the slaveholder, in cases not a few, sustains to his slaves the double relation of master and father.

I know of such cases; and it is worthy of remark that such slaves invariably suffer greater hardships, and have more to contend with, than others. They are, in the first place, a constant offence to their mistress. She is ever disposed to find fault with them; they can seldom do any thing to please her; she is never better pleased than when she sees them under the lash, especially when she suspects her husband of showing to his mulatto children favors which he withholds from his black slaves. The master is frequently compelled to sell this class of his slaves, out of deference to the feelings of his white wife; and, cruel as the deed may strike any one to be, for a man to sell his own children to human flesh-mongers, it is often the dictate of humanity for him to do so; for, unless he does this, he must not only whip them himself, but must stand by and see one white son tie up his brother, of but few shades darker complexion than himself, and ply the gory lash to his naked back; and if he lisp one word of disapproval, it is set down to his parental partiality, and only makes a bad matter worse, both for himself and the slave whom he would protect and defend.

Every year brings with it multitudes of this class of slaves. It was doubtless in consequence of a knowledge of this fact, that one great statesman of the south predicted the downfall of slavery by the inevitable laws of population. Whether this prophecy is ever fulfilled, or not, it is nevertheless plain that a very different-looking class of people are springing up at the south, and are now held in slavery, from those originally brought to this country from Africa; and if their increase will do no other good, it will do away with the force of the argument, that God cursed Ham, and therefore American slavery is right. If the lineal descendants of Ham are alone to be scripturally enslaved, it is certain that slavery at the south must soon become unscriptural; for thousands are ushered into the world, annually, who, like myself, owe their existence to white fathers, and those fathers most frequently their own masters.

I have had two masters. My first master's name was Anthony. I do not remember his first name. He was generally called Captain Anthony—a title which, I presume, he acquired by sailing a craft on the Chesapeake Bay. He was not considered a rich slaveholder. He owned two or three farms, and about thirty slaves. His farms and slaves were under the care of an overseer. The overseer's name was Plummer. Mr. Plummer was a miserable drunkard, a profane swearer, and a savage monster. He always went armed with a cowskin and a heavy cudgel. I have known him to cut and slash the women's heads so horribly, that even master would be enraged at his cruelty, and would threaten to whip him if he did not mind himself. Master, however, was not a humane slaveholder. It required extraordinary barbarity on the part of an overseer to affect him. He was a cruel man, hardened by a long life of slaveholding. He would at times seem to take great pleasure in whipping a slave. I have often been awakened at the dawn of day by the most heart-rending shrieks of an own aunt of mine, whom he used to tie up to a joist, and whip upon her naked back till she was literally covered with blood. No words, no tears, no prayers, from his gory victim, seemed to move his iron heart from its bloody purpose. The louder she screamed, the harder he whipped; and where the blood ran fastest, there he whipped longest. He would whip her to make her scream, and whip her to make her hush; and not until overcome by fatigue, would he cease to swing the blood-clotted cowskin. I remember the first time I ever witnessed this horrible exhibition. I was quite a child, but I well remember it. I never shall forget it whilst I remember any thing. It was the first of a long series of such outrages, of which I was doomed to be a witness and a participant. It struck me with awful force. It was the blood-stained gate, the entrance to the hell of slavery, through which I was about to pass. It was a most terrible spectacle. I wish I could commit to paper the feelings with which I beheld it.

This occurrence took place very soon after I went to live with my old master, and under the following circumstances. Aunt Hester went out one night,—where or for what I do not know,—and happened to be absent when my master desired her presence. He had ordered her not to go out evenings, and warned her that she must never let him catch her in company with a young man, who was paying attention to her, belonging to Colonel Lloyd. The young man's name was Ned Roberts, generally called Lloyd's Ned. Why master was so careful of her, may be safely left to conjecture. She was a woman of noble form, and of graceful proportions, having very few equals, and fewer superiors, in personal appearance, among the colored or white women of our neighborhood.

Aunt Hester had not only disobeyed his orders in going out, but had been found in company with Lloyd's Ned; which circumstance, I found, from what he said while whipping her, was the chief offence. Had he been a man of pure morals himself, he might have been thought interested in protecting the innocence of my aunt; but those who knew him will not suspect him of any such virtue. Before he commenced whipping Aunt Hester, he took her into the kitchen, and stripped her from neck to waist, leaving her neck, shoulders, and back, entirely naked. He then told her to cross her hands, calling her at the same time a d—d b—h. After crossing her hands, he tied them with a strong rope, and led her to a stool under a large hook in the joist, put in for the purpose. He made her get upon the stool, and tied her hands to the hook. She now stood fair for his infernal purpose. Her arms were stretched up at their full length, so that she stood upon the ends of her toes. He then said to her, "Now, you d—d b—h, I'll learn you how to disobey my orders!" and after rolling up his sleeves, be commenced to lay on the heavy cowskin, and soon the warm, red blood (amid heart-rending shrieks from her, and horrid oaths from him) came dripping to the floor. I was so terrified and horror-stricken at the sight, that I hid myself in a closet, and dared not venture out till long after the bloody transaction was over. I expected it would be my turn next. It was all new to me. I had never seen any thing like it before. I had always lived with my grandmother on the outskirts of the plantation, where she was put to raise the children of the younger women. I had therefore been, until now, out of the way of the bloody scenes that often occurred on the plantation.

CHAPTER II

MY MASTER'S family consisted of two sons, Andrew and Richard; one daughter, Lucretia, and her husband, Captain Thomas Auld. They lived in one house, upon the home plantation of Colonel Edward Lloyd. My master was Colonel Lloyd's clerk and superintendent. He was what might be called the overseer of the overseers. I spent two years of childhood on this plantation in my old master's family. It was here that I witnessed the bloody transaction recorded in the first chapter; and as I received my first impressions of slavery on this plantation, I will give some description of it, and of slavery as it there existed. The plantation is about twelve miles north of Easton, in Talbot county, and is situated on the border of Miles River. The principal products raised upon it were tobacco, corn, and wheat. These were raised in great abundance; so that, with the products of this and the other farms belonging to him, he was able to keep in almost constant employment a large sloop, in carrying them to market at Baltimore. This sloop was named Sally Lloyd, in honor of one of the colonel's daughters. My master's son-in-law, Captain Auld, was master of the vessel; she was otherwise manned by the colonel's own slaves. Their names were Peter, Isaac, Rich, and Jake. These were esteemed very highly by the other slaves, and looked upon as the privileged ones of the plantation; for it was no small affair, in the eyes of the slaves, to be allowed to see Baltimore.

Colonel Lloyd kept from three to four hundred slaves on his home plantation, and owned a large number more on the neighboring farms belonging to him. The names of the farms nearest to the home plantation were Wye Town and New Design. "Wye Town" was under the overseership of a man named Noah Willis. New Design was under the overseership of a Mr. Townsend. The overseers of these, and all the rest of the farms, numbering over twenty, received advice and direction from the managers of the home plantation. This was the great business place. It was the seat of government for the whole twenty farms. All disputes among the overseers were settled here. If a slave was convicted of any high misdemeanor, became unmanageable, or evinced a determination to run away, he was brought immediately here, severely whipped, put on board the sloop, carried to Baltimore, and sold to Austin Woolfolk, or some other slave-trader, as a warning to the slaves remaining.

Here, too, the slaves of all the other farms received their monthly allowance of food, and their yearly clothing. The men and women slaves received, as their monthly allowance of food, eight pounds of pork, or its equivalent in fish, and one bushel of corn meal Their yearly clothing consisted of two coarse linen shirts, one pair of linen trousers, like the shirts, one jacket, one pair of trousers for winter, made of coarse negro cloth, one pair of stockings, and one pair of shoes; the whole of which could not have cost more than seven dollars. The allowance of the slave children was given to their mothers, or the old women having the care of them. The children unable to work in the field had neither shoes, stockings, jackets, nor trousers, given to them; their clothing consisted of two coarse linen shirts per year. When these failed them, they went naked until the next allowance-day. Children from seven to ten years old, of both sexes, almost naked, might be seen at all seasons of the year.

There were no beds given the slaves, unless one coarse blanket be considered such, and none but the men and women had these. This, however, is not considered a very great privation. They find less difficulty from the want of beds, than from the want of time to sleep; for when their day's work in the field is done, the most of them having their washing, mending, and cooking to do, and having few or none of the ordinary facilities for doing either of these, very many of their sleeping hours are consumed in preparing for the field the coming day; and when this is done, old and young, male and female, married and single, drop down side by side, on one common bed,—the cold, damp floor,—each covering himself or herself with their miserable blankets; and here they sleep till they are summoned to the field by the driver's horn. At the sound of this, all must rise, and be off to the field. There must be no halting; every one must be at his or her post; and woe betides them who hear not this morning summons to the field; for if they are not awakened by the sense of hearing, they are by the sense of feeling: no age nor sex finds any favor. Mr. Severe, the overseer, used to stand by the door of the quarter, armed with a large hickory stick and heavy cowskin, ready to whip any one who was so unfortunate as not to hear, or, from any other cause, was prevented from being ready to start for the field at the sound of the horn.

Mr. Severe was rightly named: he was a cruel man. I have seen him whip a woman, causing the blood to run half an hour at the time; and this, too, in the midst of her crying children, pleading for their mother's release. He seemed to take pleasure in manifesting his fiendish barbarity. Added to his cruelty, he was a profane swearer. It was enough to chill the blood and stiffen the hair of an ordinary man to hear him talk. Scarce a sentence escaped him but that was commenced or concluded by some horrid oath. The field was the place to witness his cruelty and profanity. His presence made it both the field of blood and of blasphemy. From the rising till the going down of the sun, he was cursing, raving, cutting, and slashing among the slaves of the field, in the most frightful manner. His career was short. He died very soon after I went to Colonel Lloyd's; and he died as he lived, uttering, with his dying groans, bitter curses and horrid oaths. His death was regarded by the slaves as the result of a merciful providence.

Mr. Severe's place was filled by a Mr. Hopkins. He was a very different man. He was less cruel, less profane, and made less noise, than Mr. Severe. His course was characterized by no extraordinary demonstrations of cruelty. He whipped, but seemed to take no pleasure in it. He was called by the slaves a good overseer.

The home plantation of Colonel Lloyd wore the appearance of a country village. All the mechanical operations for all the farms were performed here. The shoemaking and mending, the blacksmithing, cartwrighting, coopering, weaving, and grain-grinding, were all performed by the slaves on the home plantation. The whole place wore a business-like aspect very unlike the neighboring farms. The number of houses, too, conspired to give it advantage over the neighboring farms. It was called by the slaves the *Great House Farm.* Few privileges were esteemed higher, by the slaves of the out-farms, than that of being selected to do errands at the Great House Farm. It was associated in their minds with greatness. A representative could not be prouder of his election to a seat in the American Congress, than a slave on one of the out-farms would be of his election to do errands at the Great House Farm. They regarded it as evidence of great confidence reposed in them by their overseers; and it was on this account, as well as a constant desire to be out of the field from under the driver's lash, that they esteemed it a high privilege, one worth careful living for. He was called the smartest and most trusty fellow, who had this honor conferred upon him the most frequently. The competitors for this office sought as diligently to please their overseers, as the office-seekers in the political parties seek to please and deceive the people. The same traits of character might be seen in Colonel Lloyd's slaves, as are seen in the slaves of the political parties.

The slaves selected to go to the Great House Farm, for the monthly allowance for themselves and their fellow-slaves, were peculiarly enthusiastic. While on their way, they would make the dense old woods, for miles around, reverberate with their wild songs, revealing at once the highest joy and the deepest sadness. They would compose and sing as they went along, consulting neither time nor tune. The thought that came up, came out—if not in the word, in the sound; —and as frequently in the one as in the other. They would sometimes sing the most pathetic sentiment in the most rapturous tone, and the most rapturous sentiment in the most pathetic tone. Into all of their songs they would manage to weave something of the Great House Farm. Especially would they do this, when leaving home. They would then sing most exultingly the following words:—

"I am going away to the Great House Farm!
O, yea! O, yea! O!"

This they would sing, as a chorus, to words which to many would seem unmeaning jargon, but which, nevertheless, were full of meaning to themselves. I have sometimes thought that the mere hearing of those songs would do more to impress some minds with the horrible character of slavery, than the reading of whole volumes of philosophy on the subject could do.

I did not, when a slave, understand the deep meaning of those rude and apparently incoherent songs. I was myself within the circle; so that I neither saw nor heard as those without might see and hear. They told a tale of woe which was then altogether beyond my feeble comprehension; they were tones loud, long, and deep; they breathed the prayer and complaint of souls boiling over with the bitterest anguish. Every tone was a testimony against slavery, and a prayer to God for deliverance from chains. The hearing of those wild notes always depressed my spirit, and filled me with ineffable sadness. I have frequently found myself in tears while hearing them. The mere recurrence to those songs, even now, afflicts me; and while I am writing these lines, an expression of feeling has already found its way down my cheek. To those songs I trace my first glimmering conception of the dehumanizing character of slavery. I can never get rid of that conception. Those songs still follow me, to deepen my hatred of slavery, and quicken my sympathies for my brethren in bonds. If any one wishes to be impressed with the soul-killing effects of slavery, let him go to Colonel Lloyd's plantation, and, on allowance-day, place himself in the deep pine woods, and there let him, in silence, analyze the sounds that shall pass through the chambers of his soul,—and if he is not thus impressed, it will only be because "there is no flesh in his obdurate heart."

I have often been utterly astonished, since I came to the north, to find persons who could speak of the singing, among slaves, as evidence of their contentment and happiness. It is impossible to conceive of a greater mistake. Slaves sing most when they are most unhappy. The songs of the slave represent the sorrows of his heart; and he is relieved by them, only as an aching heart is relieved by its tears. At least, such is my experience. I have often sung to drown my sorrow, but seldom to express my happiness. Crying for joy, and singing for joy, were alike uncommon to me while in the jaws of slavery. The singing of a man cast away upon a desolate island might be as appropriately considered as evidence of contentment and happiness, as the singing of a slave; the songs of the one and of the other are prompted by the same emotion.

CHAPTER III

COLONEL LLOYD kept a large and finely cultivated garden, which afforded almost constant employment for four
men, besides the chief gardener, (Mr. M'Durmond.) This
garden was probably the greatest attraction of the place.
During the summer months, people came from far and
near—from Baltimore, Easton, and Annapolis—to see it.
It abounded in fruits of almost every description, from
the hardy apple of the north to the delicate orange of the
south. This garden was not the least source of trouble on
the plantation. Its excellent fruit was quite a temptation
to the hungry swarms of boys, as well as the older slaves,
belonging to the colonel, few of whom had the virtue or
the vice to resist it. Scarcely a day passed, during the summer, but that some slave had to take the lash for stealing
fruit. The colonel had to resort to all kinds of stratagems
to keep his slaves out of the garden. The last most successful one was that of tarring his fence all around; after
which, if a slave was caught with any tar upon his person,
it was deemed sufficient proof that he had either been into
the garden, or had tried to get in. In either case, he was
severely whipped by the chief gardener. This plan worked
well; the slaves became as fearful of tar as of the lash. They

seemed to realize the impossibility of touching *tar* without being defiled.

The colonel also kept a splendid riding equipage. His stable and carriage-house presented the appearance of some of our large city livery establishments. His horses were of the finest form and noblest blood. His carriage-house contained three splendid coaches, three or four gigs, besides dearborns and barouches of the most fashionable style.

This establishment was under the care of two slaves—old Barney and young Barney—father and son. To attend to this establishment was their sole work. But it was by no means an easy employment; for in nothing was Colonel Lloyd more particular than in the management of his horses. The slightest inattention to these was unpardonable, and was visited upon those, under whose care they were placed, with the severest punishment; no excuse could shield them, if the colonel only suspected any want of attention to his horses—a supposition which he frequently indulged, and one which, of course, made the office of old and young Barney a very trying one. They never knew when they were safe from punishment. They were frequently whipped when least deserving, and escaped whipping when most deserving it. Every thing depended upon the looks of the horses, and the state of Colonel Lloyd's own mind when his horses were brought to him for use. If a horse did not move fast enough, or hold his head high enough, it was owing to some fault of his keepers. It was painful to stand near the stable-door, and hear the various complaints against the keepers when a horse was taken out for use. "This horse has not had proper attention. He has not been sufficiently rubbed and curried, or he has not been properly fed; his food was too wet or too dry; he got it too soon or too late; he was too hot or too cold; he had too much hay, and not enough of grain; or he had too much grain, and not enough of hay; instead of old Barney's attending to the horse, he had very improperly left it to his son." To all these complaints, no matter how unjust, the slave must answer never a word. Colonel Lloyd could not brook any contradiction from a slave. When he spoke, a slave must stand, listen, and tremble; and such was literally the case. I have seen Colonel Lloyd make old Barney, a man between fifty and sixty years of age, uncover his bald head, kneel down upon the cold, damp ground, and receive upon his naked and toil-worn shoulders more than thirty lashes at the time. Colonel Lloyd had three sons—Edward, Murray, and Daniel,—and three sons-in-law, Mr. Winder, Mr. Nicholson, and Mr. Lowndes. All of these lived at the Great House Farm, and enjoyed the luxury of whipping the servants when they pleased, from old Barney down to William Wilkes, the coach-driver. I have seen Winder make one of the house-servants stand off from him a suitable distance to be touched with the end of his whip, and at every stroke raise great ridges upon his back.

To describe the wealth of Colonel Lloyd would be almost equal to describing the riches of Job. He kept from ten to fifteen house-servants. He was said to own a thousand slaves, and I think this estimate quite within the truth. Colonel Lloyd owned so many that he did not know them when he saw them; nor did all the slaves of the out-farms know him. It is reported of him, that, while riding along the road one day, he met a colored man, and addressed him in the usual manner of speaking to colored people on the public highways of the south: "Well, boy, whom do you belong to?" "To Colonel Lloyd," replied the slave. "Well, does the colonel treat you well?" "No, sir," was the ready reply. "What, does he work you too hard?" "Yea, sir." "Well, don't he give you enough to eat?" "Yes, sir, he gives me enough, such as it is."

The colonel, after ascertaining where the slave belonged, rode on; the man also went on about his business, not dreaming that be had been conversing with his master. He thought, said, and heard nothing more of the matter, until two or three weeks afterwards. The poor man was then informed by his overseer that, for having found fault with his master, he was now to be sold to a Georgia trader. He was immediately chained and handcuffed; and thus, without a moment's warning, he was snatched away, and forever sundered, from his family and friends, by a hand more unrelenting than death. This is the penalty of telling the truth, of telling the simple truth, in answer to a series of plain questions.

It is partly in consequence of such facts, that slaves, when inquired of as to their condition and the character of their masters, almost universally say they are contented, and that their masters are kind. The slaveholders have been known to send in spies among their slaves, to ascertain their views and feelings in regard to their condition. The frequency of this has had the effect to establish among the slaves the maxim, that a still tongue makes a wise head. They suppress the truth rather than take the consequences of telling it, and in so doing prove themselves a part of the human family. If they have any thing to say of their masters, it is generally in their masters' favor, especially when speaking to an untried man. I have been frequently asked, when a slave, if I had a kind master, and do not remember ever to have given a negative answer; nor did I, in pursuing this course, consider myself as uttering what was absolutely false; for I always measured the kindness of my master by the standard of kindness set up among slaveholders around us. Moreover, slaves are like other people, and imbibe prejudices quite common to others. They think their own better than that of others. Many, under the influence of this prejudice, think their own masters are better than the masters of other slaves; and this, too, in some cases, when the very reverse is true. Indeed, it is not uncommon for slaves even to fall out and quarrel among themselves about the relative goodness of their masters, each contending for the superior goodness of his own over that of the others. At the very same time, they mutually execrate their masters when viewed separately. It was so on our plantation. When Colonel Lloyd's slaves met the slaves of Jacob Jepson, they seldom parted without a quarrel about their masters; Colonel Lloyd's slaves contending that he was the richest, and Mr. Jepson's slaves that he was the smartest, and most of a man. Colonel Lloyd's slaves would boast his ability to buy and sell Jacob Jepson. Mr. Jepson's slaves would boast his ability to whip Colonel Lloyd. These quarrels would almost always end in a fight between the parties, and those that whipped were supposed to have gained the point at issue. They seemed to think that the greatness of their masters was transferable to themselves. It was considered as being bad enough to be a slave; but to be a poor man's slave was deemed a disgrace indeed!

CHAPTER IV

MR. HOPKINS remained but a short time in the office of overseer. Why his career was so short, I do not know, but suppose he lacked the necessary severity to suit Colonel Lloyd. Mr. Hopkins was succeeded by Mr. Austin Gore, a man possessing, in an eminent degree, all those traits of character indispensable to what is called a first-rate overseer. Mr. Gore had served Colonel Lloyd, in the capacity of overseer, upon one of the out-farms, and had shown himself worthy of the high station of overseer upon the home or Great House Farm.

Mr. Gore was proud, ambitious, and persevering. He was artful, cruel, and obdurate. He was just the man for such a place, and it was just the place for such a man. It afforded scope for the full exercise of all his powers, and he seemed to be perfectly at home in it. He was one of those who could torture the slightest look, word, or gesture, on the part of the slave, into impudence, and would treat it accordingly. There must be no answering back to him; no explanation was allowed a slave, showing himself to have been wrongfully accused. Mr. Gore acted fully up to the maxim laid down by slaveholders,—"It is better that a dozen slaves suffer under the lash, than that the overseer should be convicted, in the presence of the slaves, of having been at fault." No matter how innocent a slave might be—it availed him nothing, when accused by Mr. Gore of any misdemeanor. To be accused was to be convicted, and to be convicted was to be punished; the one always following the other with immutable certainty. To escape punishment was to escape accusation; and few slaves had the fortune to do either, under the overseership of Mr. Gore. He was just proud enough to demand the most debasing homage of the slave, and quite servile enough to crouch, himself, at the feet of the master. He was ambitious enough to be contented with nothing short of the highest rank of overseers, and persevering enough to reach the height of his ambition. He was cruel enough to inflict the severest punishment, artful enough to descend to the lowest trickery, and obdurate enough to be insensible to the voice of a reproving conscience. He was, of all the overseers, the most dreaded by the slaves. His presence was painful; his eye flashed confusion; and seldom was his sharp, shrill voice heard, without producing horror and trembling in their ranks.

Mr. Gore was a grave man, and, though a young man, he indulged in no jokes, said no funny words, seldom smiled. His words were in perfect keeping with his looks, and his looks were in perfect keeping with his words. Overseers will sometimes indulge in a witty word, even with the slaves; not so with Mr. Gore. He spoke but to command, and commanded but to be obeyed; he dealt sparingly with his words, and bountifully with his whip, never using the former where the latter would answer as well. When he whipped, he seemed to do so from a sense of duty, and feared no consequences. He did nothing reluctantly, no matter how disagreeable; always at his post, never inconsistent. He never promised but to fulfil. He was, in a word, a man of the most inflexible firmness and stone-like coolness.

His savage barbarity was equaled only by the consummate coolness with which he committed the grossest and most savage deeds upon the slaves under his charge. Mr. Gore once undertook to whip one of Colonel Lloyd's slaves, by the name of Demby. He had given Demby but few stripes, when, to get rid of the scourging, he ran and plunged himself into a creek, and stood there at the depth of his shoulders, refusing to come out. Mr. Gore told him that he would give him three calls, and that, if he did not come out at the third call, he would shoot him. The first call was given. Demby made no response, but stood his ground. The second and third calls were given with the same result. Mr. Gore then, without consultation or deliberation with any one, not even giving Demby an additional call, raised his musket to his face, taking deadly aim at his standing victim, and in an instant poor Demby was no more. His mangled body sank out of sight, and blood and brains marked the water where he had stood.

A thrill of horror flashed through every soul upon the plantation, excepting Mr. Gore. He alone seemed cool and collected. He was asked by Colonel Lloyd and my old master, why he resorted to this extraordinary expedient. His reply was, (as well as I can remember,) that Demby had become unmanageable. He was setting a dangerous example to the other slaves,—one which, if suffered to pass without some such demonstration on his part, would finally lead to the total subversion of all rule and order upon the plantation. He argued that if one slave refused to be corrected, and escaped with his life, the other slaves would soon copy the example; the result of which would be, the freedom of the slaves, and the enslavement of the whites. Mr. Gore's defence was satisfactory. He was continued in his station as overseer upon the home plantation. His fame as an overseer went abroad. His horrid crime was not even submitted to judicial investigation. It was committed in the presence of slaves, and they of course could neither institute a suit, nor testify against him; and thus the guilty perpetrator of one of the bloodiest and most foul murders goes unwhipped of justice, and uncensored by the community in which he lives. Mr. Gore lived in St. Michael's, Talbot county, Maryland, when I left there; and if he is still alive, he very probably lives there now; and if so, he is now, as he was then, as highly esteemed and as much respected as though his guilty soul had not been stained with his brother's blood.

I speak advisedly when I say this,—that killing a slave, or any colored person, in Talbot county, Maryland, is not treated as a crime, either by the courts or the community. Mr.

Thomas Lanman, of St. Michael's, killed two slaves, one of whom he killed with a hatchet, by knocking his brains out. He used to boast of the commission of the awful and bloody deed. I have heard him do so laughingly, saying, among other things, that he was the only benefactor of his country in the company, and that when others would do as much as he had done, we should be relieved of "the d—d niggers."

The wife of Mr. Giles Hick, living but a short distance from where I used to live, murdered my wife's cousin, a young girl between fifteen and sixteen years of age, mangling her person in the most horrible manner, breaking her nose and breastbone with a stick, so that the poor girl expired in a few hours afterward. She was immediately buried, but had not been in her untimely grave but a few hours before she was taken up and examined by the coroner, who decided that she had come to her death by severe beating. The offence for which this girl was thus murdered was this:— She had been set that night to mind Mrs. Hick's baby, and during the night she fell asleep, and the baby cried. She, having lost her rest for several nights previous, did not hear the crying. They were both in the room with Mrs. Hicks. Mrs. Hicks, finding the girl slow to move, jumped from her bed, seized an oak stick of wood by the fireplace, and with it broke the girl's nose and breastbone, and thus ended her life. I will not say that this most horrid murder produced no sensation in the community. It did produce sensation, but not enough to bring the murderess to punishment. There was a warrant issued for her arrest, but it was never served. Thus she escaped not only punishment, but even the pain of being arraigned before a court for her horrid crime.

Whilst I am detailing bloody deeds which took place during my stay on Colonel Lloyd's plantation, I will briefly narrate another, which occurred about the same time as the murder of Demby by Mr. Gore.

Colonel Lloyd's slaves were in the habit of spending a part of their nights and Sundays in fishing for oysters, and in this way made up the deficiency of their scanty allowance. An old man belonging to Colonel Lloyd, while thus engaged, happened to get beyond the limits of Colonel Lloyd's, and on the premises of Mr. Beal Bondly. At this trespass, Mr. Bondly took offence, and with his musket came down to the shore, and blew its deadly contents into the poor old man.

Mr. Bondly came over to see Colonel Lloyd the next day, whether to pay him for his property, or to justify himself in what he had done, I know not. At any rate, this whole fiendish transaction was soon hushed up. There was very little said about it at all, and nothing done. It was a common saying, even among little white boys, that it was worth a half-cent to kill a "nigger," and a half-cent to bury one.

As to my own treatment while I lived on Colonel Lloyd's plantation, it was very similar to that of the other slave children. I was not old enough to work in the field, and there being little else than field work to do, I had a great deal of leisure time. The most I had to do was to drive up the cows at evening, keep the fowls out of the garden, keep the front yard clean, and run of errands for my old master's daughter, Mrs. Lucretia Auld. The most of my leisure time I spent in helping Master Daniel Lloyd in finding his birds, after he had shot them. My connection with Master Daniel was of some advantage to me. He became quite attached to me, and was a sort of protector of me. He would not allow the older boys to impose upon me, and would divide his cakes with me.

I was seldom whipped by my old master, and suffered little from any thing else than hunger and cold. I suffered much from hunger, but much more from cold. In hottest summer and coldest winter, I was kept almost naked—no shoes, no stockings, no jacket, no trousers, nothing on but a coarse tow linen shirt, reaching only to my knees. I had no bed. I must have perished with cold, but that, the coldest nights, I used to steal a bag which was used for carrying corn to the mill. I would crawl into this bag, and there sleep on the cold, damp, clay floor, with my head in and feet out. My feet have been so cracked with the frost that the pen with which I am writing might be laid in the gashes.

We were not regularly allowanced. Our food was coarse corn meal boiled. This was called *mush*. It was put into a large wooden tray or trough, and set down upon the ground. The children were then called, like so many pigs, and like so many pigs they would come and devour the mush; some with oyster-shells, others with pieces of shingle, some with naked hands, and none with spoons. He that ate fastest got most; he that was strongest secured the best place; and few left the trough satisfied.

I was probably between seven and eight years old when I left Colonel Lloyd's plantation. I left it with joy. I shall never forget the ecstasy with which I received the intelligence that my old master (Anthony) had determined to let me go to Baltimore, to live with Mr. Hugh Auld, brother to my old master's son-in-law, Captain Thomas Auld. I received this information about three days before my departure. They were three of the happiest days I ever enjoyed. I spent the most part of all these three days in the creek, washing off the plantation scurf, and preparing myself for my departure.

The pride of appearance which this would indicate was not my own. I spent the time in washing, not so much because I wished to, but because Mrs. Lucretia had told me I must get all the dead skin off my feet and knees before I could go to Baltimore; for the people in Baltimore were very cleanly, and would laugh at me if I looked dirty. Besides, she was going to give me a pair or trousers, which I should not put on unless I got all the dirt off me. The thought of owning a pair of trousers was great indeed! It was almost a sufficient motive, not only to make me take off what would be called by pig-drovers the mange, but the skin itself. I went at it in good earnest, working for the first time with the hope of reward.

The ties that ordinarily bind children to their homes were all suspended in my case. I found no severe trial in my departure. My home was charmless; it was not home to me; on parting from it, I could not feel that I was leaving any thing which I could have enjoyed by staying. My mother was dead, my grandmother lived far off, so that I seldom saw her. I had two sisters and one brother, that lived in the same house with me; but the early separation of us from our mother had well nigh blotted the fact of our relationship from our memories. I looked for home elsewhere, and was confident of finding none which I should relish less than the one which I was leaving. If, however, I found in my new home hardship, hunger, whipping, and nakedness, I had the consolation that I should not have escaped any one of them by staying. Having already had more than a taste of them in the house of my old master, and having endured them there, I very naturally inferred my ability to endure them elsewhere, and especially at Baltimore; for I had something of the feeling about Baltimore that is expressed in the proverb, that "being hanged in England is preferable to dying a natural death in Ireland." I had the strongest desire to see Baltimore. Cousin Tom, though not fluent in speech, had inspired me with that desire by his eloquent description of the place. I could never point out any thing at the Great House, no matter how beautiful or powerful, but that he had seen something at Baltimore far exceeding, both in beauty and strength, the object which I pointed out to him. Even the Great House itself, with all its pictures, was far inferior to many buildings in Baltimore. So strong was my desire, that I thought a gratification of it would fully compensate for whatever loss of comforts I should sustain by the exchange. I left without a regret, and with the highest hopes of future happiness.

We sailed out of Miles River for Baltimore on a Saturday morning. I remember only the day of the week, for at that time I had no knowledge of the days of the month, nor the months of the year. On setting sail, I walked aft, and gave to Colonel Lloyd's plantation what I hoped would be the last look. I then placed myself in the bows of the sloop, and there spent the remainder of the day in looking ahead, interesting myself in what was in the distance rather than in things nearby or behind.

In the afternoon of that day, we reached Annapolis, the capital of the State. We stopped but a few moments so that I had no time to go on shore. It was the first large town that

I had ever seen, and though it would look small compared with some of our New England factory villages, I thought it a wonderful place for its size—more imposing even than the Great House Farm!

We arrived at Baltimore early on Sunday morning, landing at Smith's Wharf, not far from Bowley's Wharf. We had on board the sloop a large flock of sheep; and after aiding in driving them to the slaughterhouse of Mr. Curtis on Louden Slater's Hill, I was conducted by Rich, one of the hands belonging on board of the sloop, to my new home in Alliciana Street, near Mr. Gardner's ship-yard, on Fells Point.

Mr. and Mrs. Auld were both at home, and met me at the door with their little son Thomas, to take care of whom I had been given. And here I saw what I had never seen before; it was a white face beaming with the most kindly emotions; it was the face of my new mistress, Sophia Auld. I wish I could describe the rapture that flashed through my soul as I beheld it. It was a new and strange sight to me, brightening up my pathway with the light of happiness. Little Thomas was told, there was his Freddy,—and I was told to take care of little Thomas; and thus I entered upon the duties of my new home with the most cheering prospect ahead.

I look upon my departure from Colonel Lloyd's plantation as one of the most interesting events of my life. It is possible, and even quite probable, that but for the mere circumstance of being removed from that plantation to Baltimore, I should have to-day, instead of being here seated by my own table, in the enjoyment of freedom and the happiness of home, writing this Narrative, been confined in the galling chains of slavery. Going to live at Baltimore laid the foundation, and opened the gateway, to all my subsequent prosperity. I have ever regarded it as the first plain manifestation of that kind providence which has ever since attended me, and marked my life with so many favors. I regarded the selection of myself as being somewhat remarkable. There were a number of slave children that might have been sent from the plantation to Baltimore. There were those younger, those older, and those of the same age. I was chosen from among them all, and was the first, last, and only choice.

I may be deemed superstitions, and even egotistical, in regarding this event as a special interposition of divine Providence in my favor. But I should be false to the earliest sentiments of my soul, if I suppressed the opinion. I prefer to be true to myself, even at the hazard of incurring the ridicule of others, rather than to be false, and incur my own abhorrence. From my earliest recollection, I date the entertainment of a deep conviction that slavery would not always be able to hold me within its foul embrace; and in the darkest hours of my career in slavery, this living word of faith and spirit of hope departed not from me, but remained like ministering angels to cheer me through the gloom. This good spirit was from God, and to him I offer thanksgiving and praise.

CHAPTER VI

My new mistress proved to be all she appeared when I first met her at the door,—a woman of the kindest heart and finest feelings. She had never had a slave under her control previously to myself, and prior to her marriage she had been dependent upon her own industry for a living. She was by trade a weaver; and by constant application to her business, she had been in a good degree preserved from the blighting and dehumanizing effects of slavery. I was utterly astonished at her goodness. I scarcely knew how to behave towards her. She was entirely unlike any other white woman I had ever seen. I could not approach her as I was accustomed to approach other white ladies. My early instruction was all out of place. The crouching servility, usually so acceptable a quality in a slave, did not answer when manifested toward her. Her favor was not gained by it; she seemed to be disturbed by it. She did not deem it impudent or unmannerly for a slave to look her in the face. The meanest slave was put fully at ease in her presence, and none left without feeling better for having seen her. Her face was made of heavenly smiles, and her voice of tranquil music.

But, alas! this kind heart had but a short time to remain such. The fatal poison of irresponsible power was already in her hands, and soon commenced its infernal work. That cheerful eye, under the influence of slavery, soon became red with rage; that voice, made all of sweet accord, changed to one of harsh and horrid discord; and that angelic face gave place to that of a demon.

Very soon after I went to live with Mr. and Mrs. Auld, she very kindly commenced to teach me the A, B, C. After I had learned this, she assisted me in learning to spell words of three or four letters. Just at this point of my progress, Mr. Auld found out what was going on, and at once forbade Mrs. Auld to instruct me further, telling her, among other things, that it was unlawful, as well as unsafe, to teach a slave to read. To use his own words, further, he said, "If you give a nigger an inch, he will take an ell. A nigger should know nothing but to obey his master—to do as he is told to do. Learning would spoil the best nigger in the world. Now," said he, "if you teach that nigger (speaking of myself) how to read, there would be no keeping him. It would forever unfit him to be a slave. He would at once become unmanageable, and of no value to his master. As to himself, it could do him no good, but a great deal of harm. It would make him discontented and unhappy." These words sank deep into my heart, stirred up sentiments within that lay slumbering, and called into existence an entirely new train of thought. It was a new and special revelation, explaining dark and mysterious things, with which my youthful understanding had struggled, but struggled in vain. I now understood what had been to me a most perplexing difficulty—to wit, the white man's power to enslave the black man. It was a grand achievement, and I prized it highly. From that moment, I understood the pathway from slavery to freedom. It was just what I wanted, and I got it at a time when I the least expected it. Whilst I was saddened by the thought of losing the aid of my kind mistress, I was gladdened by the invaluable instruction which, by the merest accident, I had gained from my master. Though conscious of the difficulty of learning without a teacher, I set out with high hope, and a fixed purpose, at whatever cost of trouble, to learn how to read. The very decided manner with which he spoke, and strove to impress his wife with the evil consequences of giving me instruction, served to convince me that he was deeply sensible of the truths he was uttering. It gave me the best assurance that I might rely with the utmost confidence on the results which, he said, would flow from teaching me to read. What he most dreaded, that I most desired. What he most loved, that I most hated. That which to him was a great evil, to be carefully shunned, was to me a great good, to be diligently sought; and the argument which he so warmly urged, against my learning to read, only served to inspire me with a desire and determination to learn. In learning to read, I owe almost as much to the bitter opposition of my master, as to the kindly aid of my mistress. I acknowledge the benefit of both.

I had resided but a short time in Baltimore before I

observed a marked difference, in the treatment of slaves, from that which I had witnessed in the country. A city slave is almost a freeman, compared with a slave on the plantation. He is much better fed and clothed, and enjoys privileges altogether unknown to the slave on the plantation. There is a vestige of decency, a sense of shame, that does much to curb and check those outbreaks of atrocious cruelty so commonly enacted upon the plantation. He is a desperate slaveholder, who will shock the humanity of his non-slave-holding neighbors with the cries of his lacerated slave. Few are willing to incur the odium attaching to the reputation of being a cruel master; and above all things, they would not be known as not giving a slave enough to eat. Every city slaveholder is anxious to have it known of him, that he feeds his slaves well; and it is due to them to say, that most of them do give their slaves enough to eat. There are, however, some painful exceptions to this rule. Directly opposite to us, on Philpot Street, lived Mr. Thomas Hamilton. He owned two slaves. Their names were Henrietta and Mary. Henrietta was about twenty-two years of age, Mary was about fourteen; and of all the mangled and emaciated creatures I ever looked upon, these two were the most so. His heart must be harder than stone, that could look upon these unmoved. The head, neck, and shoulders of Mary were literally cut to pieces. I have frequently felt her head, and found it nearly covered with festering sores, caused by the lash of her cruel mistress. I do not know that her master ever whipped her, but I have been an eye-witness to the cruelty of Mrs. Hamilton. I used to be in Mr. Hamilton's house nearly every day. Mrs. Hamilton used to sit in a large chair in the middle of the room, with a heavy cowskin always by her side, and scarce an hour passed during the day but was marked by the blood of one of these slaves. The girls seldom passed her without her saying, "Move faster, you *black gip!*" at the same time giving them a blow with the cowskin over the head or shoulders, often drawing the blood. She would then say, "Take that, you *black gip!*"— continuing, "If you don't move faster, I'll move you!" Added to the cruel lashings to which these slaves were subjected, they were kept nearly half-starved. They seldom knew what it was to eat a full meal. I have seen Mary contending with the pigs for the offal thrown into the street. So much was Mary kicked and cut to pieces, that she was oftener called *"pecked"* than by her name.

CHAPTER VII

I LIVED in Master Hugh's family about seven years. During this time, I succeeded in learning to read and write. In accomplishing this, I was compelled to resort to various stratagems. I had no regular teacher. My mistress, who had kindly commenced to instruct me, had, in compliance with the advice and direction of her husband, not only ceased to instruct, but had set her face against my being instructed by any one else. It is due, however, to my mistress to say of her, that she did not adopt this course of treatment immediately. She at first lacked the depravity indispensable to shutting me up in mental darkness. It was at least necessary for her to have some training in the exercise of irresponsible power, to make her equal to the task of treating me as though I were a brute.

My mistress was, as I have said, a kind and tender-hearted woman; and in the simplicity of her soul she commenced, when I first went to live with her, to treat me as she supposed one human being ought to treat another. In entering upon the duties of a slaveholder, she did not seem to perceive that I sustained to her the relation of a mere chattel, and that for her to treat me as a human being was not only wrong, but dangerously so. Slavery proved as injurious to her as it did to me. When I went there, she was a pious, warm, and tender-hearted woman. There was no sorrow or suffering for which she had not a tear. She had bread for the hungry, clothes for the naked, and comfort for every mourner that came within her reach. Slavery soon proved its ability to divest her of these heavenly qualities. Under its influence, the tender heart became stone, and the lamblike disposition gave way to one of tiger-like fierceness. The first step in her downward course was in her ceasing to instruct me. She now commenced to practise her husband's precepts. She finally became even more violent in her opposition than her husband himself. She was not satisfied with simply doing as well as he had commanded; she seemed anxious to do better. Nothing seemed to make her more angry than to see me with a newspaper. She seemed to think that here lay the danger. I have had her rush at me with a face made all up of fury, and snatch from me a newspaper, in a manner that fully revealed her apprehension. She was an apt woman; and a little experience soon demonstrated, to her satisfaction, that education and slavery were incompatible with each other.

From this time I was most narrowly watched. If I was in a separate room any considerable length of time, I was sure to be suspected of having a book, and was at once called to give an account of myself. All this, however, was too late. The first step had been taken. Mistress, in teaching me the alphabet, had given me the *inch*, and no precaution could prevent me from taking the *ell*.

The plan which I adopted, and the one by which I was most successful, was that of making friends of all the little white boys whom I met in the street. As many of these as I could, I converted into teachers. With their kindly aid, obtained at different times and in different places, I finally succeeded in learning to read. When I was sent of errands, I always took my book with me, and by going one part of my errand quickly, I found time to get a lesson before my return. I used also to carry bread with me, enough of which was always in the house, and to which I was always welcome; for I was much better off in this regard than many of the poor white children in our neighborhood. This bread I used to bestow upon the hungry little urchins, who, in return, would give me that more valuable bread of knowledge. I am strongly tempted to give the names of two or three of those little boys, as a testimonial of the gratitude and affection I bear them; but prudence forbids;—not that it would injure me, but it might embarrass them; for it is almost an unpardonable offence to teach slaves to read in this Christian country. It is enough to say of the dear little fellows, that they lived on Philpot Street, very near Durgin and Bailey's shipyard. I used to talk this matter of slavery over with them. I would sometimes say to them, I wished I could be as free as they would be when they got to be men. "You will be free as soon as you are twenty-one, *but I am a slave for life!* Have not I as good a right to be free as you have?" These words used to trouble them; they would express for me the liveliest sympathy, and console me with the hope that something would occur by which I might be free.

I was now about twelve years old, and the thought of being *a slave for life* began to bear heavily upon my heart. Just about this time, I got hold of a book entitled "The Columbian Orator." Every opportunity I got, I used to read this book. Among much of other interesting matter, I found in it a dialogue between a master and his slave. The slave was represented as having run away from his master three times. The dialogue represented the conversation which took place between them, when the slave was retaken the third time. In this dialogue, the whole argument in behalf of slavery was brought forward by the master, all of which was disposed of by the slave. The slave was made to say some very smart as well as impressive things in reply to his master—things which had the desired though unexpected effect; for the conversation resulted in the voluntary emancipation of the slave on the part of the master.

In the same book, I met with one of Sheridan's mighty speeches on and in behalf of Catholic emancipation. These were choice documents to me. I read them over and over again with unabated interest. They gave tongue to interesting thoughts of my own soul, which had frequently flashed through my mind, and died away for want of utterance. The moral which I gained from the dialogue was the power of truth over the conscience of even a slaveholder. What I got from Sheridan was a bold denunciation of slavery, and a powerful vindication of human rights. The reading of these documents enabled me to utter my thoughts, and to meet the arguments brought forward to sustain slavery; but while they relieved me of one difficulty, they brought on another even more painful than the one of which I was relieved. The more I read, the more I was led to abhor and detest my enslavers. I could regard them in no other light than a band of successful robbers, who had left their homes, and gone to Africa, and stolen us from our homes, and in a strange land reduced us to slavery. I loathed them as being the meanest as well as the most wicked of men. As I read and contemplated the subject, behold! that very discontentment which Master Hugh had predicted would follow my learning to read had already come, to torment and sting my soul to unutterable anguish. As I writhed under it, I would at times feel that learning to read had been a curse rather than a blessing. It had given me a view of my wretched condition, without the remedy. It opened my eyes to the horrible pit, but to no ladder upon which to get out. In moments of agony, I envied my fellow-slaves for their stupidity. I have often wished myself a beast. I preferred the condition of the meanest reptile to my own. Any thing, no matter what, to get rid of thinking! It was this everlasting thinking of my condition that tormented me. There was no getting rid of it. It was pressed upon me by every object within sight or hearing, animate or inanimate. The silver trump of freedom had roused my soul to eternal wakefulness. Freedom now appeared, to disappear no more forever. It was heard in every sound, and seen in every thing. It was ever present to torment me with a sense of my wretched condition. I saw nothing without seeing it, I heard nothing without hearing it, and felt nothing without feeling it. It looked from every star, it smiled in every calm, breathed in every wind, and moved in every storm.

I often found myself regretting my own existence, and wishing myself dead; and but for the hope of being free, I have no doubt but that I should have killed myself, or done something for which I should have been killed. While in this state of mind, I was eager to hear any one speak of slavery. I was a ready listener. Every little while, I could hear something about the abolitionists. It was some time before I found what the word meant. It was always used in such connections as to make it an interesting word to me. If a slave ran away and succeeded in getting clear, or if a slave killed his master, set fire to a barn, or did any thing very wrong in the mind of a slaveholder, it was spoken of as the fruit of *abolition*. Hearing the word in this connection very often, I set about learning what it meant. The dictionary afforded me little or no help. I found it was "the act of abolishing;" but then I did not know what was to be abolished. Here I was perplexed. I did not dare to ask any one about its meaning, for I was satisfied that it was something they wanted me to know very little about. After a patient waiting, I got one of our city papers, containing an account of the number of petitions from the north, praying for the abolition of slavery in the District of Columbia, and of the slave trade between the States. From this time I understood the words *abolition* and *abolitionist*, and always drew near when that word was spoken, expecting to bear something of importance to myself and fellow-slaves. The light broke in upon me by degrees. I went one day down on the wharf of Mr. Waters; and seeing two Irishmen unloading a scow of stone, I went, unasked, and helped them. When we had finished, one of them came to me and asked me if I were a slave. I told him I was. He asked, "Are ye a slave for life?" I told him that I was. The good Irishman seemed to be deeply affected by the statement. He said to the other that it was a pity so fine a little fellow as myself should be a slave for life. He said it was a shame to hold me. They both advised me to run away to the north; that I should find friends there, and that I should be free. I pretended not to be interested in what they said, and treated them as if I did not understand them; for I feared they might be treacherous. White men have been known to encourage slaves to escape, and then, to get the reward, catch them and return them to their masters. I was afraid that these seemingly good men might use me so; but I nevertheless remembered their advice, and from that time I resolved to run away. I looked forward to a time at which it would be safe for me to escape. I was too young to think of doing so immediately; besides, I wished to learn how to write, as I might have occasion to write my own pass.

I consoled myself with the hope that I should one day find a good chance. Meanwhile, I would learn to write.

The idea as to how I might learn to write was suggested to me by being in Durgin and Bailey's ship-yard, and frequently seeing the ship carpenters, after hewing, and getting a piece of timber ready for use, write on the timber the name of that part of the ship for which it was intended. When a piece of timber was intended for the larboard side, it would be marked thus—"L." When a piece was for the starboard side, it would be marked thus— "S." A piece for the larboard side forward, would be marked thus—"L. F." When a piece was for starboard side forward, it would be marked thus—"S. F." For larboard aft, it would be marked thus—"L. A." For starboard aft, it would be marked thus—"S. A." I soon learned the names of these letters, and for what they were intended when placed upon a piece of timber in the ship-yard. I immediately commenced copying them, and in a short time was able to make the four letters named. After that, when I met with any boy who I knew could write, I would tell him I could write as well as he. The next word would be, "I don't believe you. Let me see you try it." I would then make the letters which I had been so fortunate as to learn, and ask him to beat that. In this way I got a good many lessons in writing, which it is quite possible I should never have gotten in any other way. During this time, my copy-book was the board fence, brick wall, and pavement; my pen and ink was a lump of chalk. With these, I learned mainly how to write. I then commenced and continued copying the Italics in Webster's Spelling Book, until I could make them all without looking on the book. By this time, my little Master Thomas had gone to school, and learned how to write, and had written over a number of copy-books. These had been brought home, and shown to some of our near neighbors, and then laid aside. My mistress used to go to class meeting at the Wilk Street meeting house every Monday afternoon, and leave me to take care of the house. When left thus, I used to spend the time in writing in the spaces left in Master Thomas's copy-book, copying what he had written. I continued to do this until I could write a hand very similar to that of Master Thomas. Thus, after a long, tedious effort for years, I finally succeeded in learning how to write.

CHAPTER VIII

In a very short time after I went to live at Baltimore, my old master's youngest son Richard died; and in about three years and six months after his death, my old master, Captain Anthony, died, leaving only his son, Andrew, and daughter, Lucretia, to share his estate. He died while on a visit to see his daughter at Hillsborough. Cut off thus unexpectedly, he left no will as to the disposal of his property. It was therefore necessary to have a valuation of the property, that it might be equally divided between Mrs. Lucretia and Master Andrew. I was immediately sent for, to be valued with the other property. Here again my feelings rose up in detestation of slavery. I had now a new conception of my degraded condition. Prior to this, I had become, if not insensible to my lot, at least partly so. I left Baltimore with a young heart overborne with sadness, and a soul full of apprehension. I took passage with Captain Rowe, in the schooner Wild Cat, and, after a sail of about twenty-four hours, I found myself near the place of my birth. I had now been absent from it almost, if not quite, five years. I, however, remembered the place very well. I was only about five years old when I left it, to go and live with my old master on Colonel Lloyd's plantation; so that I was now between ten and eleven years old.

We were all ranked together at the valuation. Men and women, old and young, married and single, were ranked with horses, sheep, and swine. There were horses and men, cattle and women, pigs and children, all holding the same rank in the scale of being, and were all subjected to the same narrow examination. Silvery-headed age and sprightly youth, maids and matrons, had to undergo the same indelicate inspection. At this moment, I saw more clearly than ever the brutalizing effects of slavery upon both slave and slaveholder.

After the valuation, then came the division. I have no language to express the high excitement and deep anxiety which were felt among us poor slaves during this time. Our fate for life was now to be decided. We had no more voice in that decision than the brutes among whom we were ranked. A single word from the white men was enough—against all our wishes, prayers, and entreaties—to sunder forever the dearest friends, dearest kindred, and strongest ties known to human beings. In addition to the pain of separation, there was the horrid dread of falling into the hands of Master Andrew. He was known to us all as being a most cruel wretch,—a common drunkard, who had, by his reckless mismanagement and profligate dissipation already wasted a large portion of his father's property. We all felt that we might as well be sold at once to the Georgia traders, as to pass into his hands; for we knew that that would be our inevitable condition,—a condition held by us all in the utmost horror and dread.

I suffered more anxiety than most of my fellow-slaves. I had known what it was to be kindly treated; they had known nothing of the kind. They had seen little or nothing of the world. They were in very deed men and women of sorrow, and acquainted with grief. Their backs had been made familiar with the bloody lash, so that they had become callous; mine was yet tender; for while at Baltimore I got few whippings, and few slaves could boast of a kinder master and mistress than myself; and the thought of passing out of their hands into those of Master Andrew—a man who, but a few days before, to give me a sample of his bloody disposition, took my little brother by the throat, threw him on the ground, and with the heel of his boot stamped upon his head till the blood gushed from his nose and ears—was well calculated to make me anxious as to my fate. After he had committed this savage outrage upon my brother, he turned to me, and said that was the way he meant to serve me one of these days,—meaning, I suppose, when I came into his possession.

Thanks to a kind Providence, I fell to the portion of Mrs. Lucretia, and was sent immediately back to Baltimore, to live again in the family of Master Hugh. Their joy at my return equalled their sorrow at my departure. It was a glad day to me. I had escaped a fate worse than lion's jaws. I was absent from Baltimore, for the purpose of valuation and division, just about one month, and it seemed to have been six.

Very soon after my return to Baltimore, my mistress,

Lucretia, died, leaving her husband and one child, Amanda; and in a very short time after her death, Master Andrew died. Now all the property of my old master, slaves included, was in the hands of strangers,—strangers who had had nothing to do with accumulating it. Not a slave was left free. All remained slaves, from the youngest to the oldest. If any one thing in my experience, more than another, served to deepen my conviction of the infernal character of slavery, and to fill me with unutterable loathing of slaveholders, it was their base ingratitude to my poor old grandmother. She had served my old master faithfully from youth to old age. She had been the source of all his wealth; she had peopled his plantation with slaves; she had become a great-grandmother in his service. She had rocked him in infancy, attended him in childhood, served him through life, and at his death wiped from his icy brow the cold death-sweat, and closed his eyes forever. She was nevertheless left a slave—a slave for life—a slave in the hands of strangers; and in their hands she saw her children, her grandchildren, and her great-grandchildren, divided, like so many sheep, without being gratified with the small privilege of a single word, as to their or her own destiny. And, to cap the climax of their base ingratitude and fiendish barbarity, my grandmother, who was now very old, having outlived my old master and all his children, having seen the beginning and end of all of them, and her present owners finding she was of but little value, her frame already racked with the pains of old age, and complete helplessness fast stealing over her once active limbs, they took her to the woods, built her a little hut, put up a little mud-chimney, and then made her welcome to the privilege of supporting herself there in perfect loneliness; thus virtually turning her out to die! If my poor old grandmother now lives, she lives to suffer in utter loneliness; she lives to remember and mourn over the loss of children, the loss of grandchildren, and the loss of great-grandchildren. They are, in the language of the slave's poet, Whittier,—

> "Gone, gone, sold and gone
>   To the rice swamp dank and lone,
>   Where the slave-whip ceaseless swings,
>   Where the noisome insect stings,
>   Where the fever-demon strews
>   Poison with the failing dews,
>   Where the sickly sunbeams glare
>   Through the hot and misty air:—
>   Gone, gone, sold and gone
>   To the rice swamp dank and lone,
>   From Virginia hills and waters—
>   Woe is me, my stolen daughters!"

The hearth is desolate. The children, the unconscious children, who once sang and danced in her presence, are gone. She gropes her way, in the darkness of age, for a drink of water. Instead of the voices of her children, she hears by day the moans of the dove, and by night the screams of the hideous owl. All is gloom. The grave is at the door. And now, when weighed down by the pains and aches of old age, when the head inclines to the feet, when the beginning and ending of human existence meet, and helpless infancy and painful old age combine together—at this time, this most needful time, the time for the exercise of that tenderness and affection which children only can exercise towards a declining parent—my poor old grandmother, the devoted mother of twelve children, is left all alone, in yonder little hut, before a few dim embers. She stands—she sits—she staggers—she falls—she groans—she dies—and there are none of her children or grandchildren present, to wipe from her wrinkled brow the cold sweat of death, or to place beneath the sod her fallen remains. Will not a righteous God visit for these things?

In about two years after the death of Mrs. Lucretia, Master Thomas married his second wife. Her name was Rowena Hamilton. She was the eldest daughter of Mr. William Hamilton. Master now lived in St. Michael's. Not long after his marriage, a misunderstanding took place between himself and Master Hugh; and as a means of punishing his brother, he took me from him to live with himself at St. Michael's. Here I underwent another most painful separation. It, however, was not so severe as the one I dreaded at the division of property; for, during this interval, a great change had taken place in Master Hugh and his once kind and affectionate wife. The influence of brandy upon him, and of slavery upon her, had effected a disastrous change in the characters of both; so that, as far as they were concerned, I thought I had little to lose by the change. But it was not to them that I was attached. It was to those little Baltimore boys that I felt the strongest attachment. I had received many good lessons from them, and was still receiving them, and the thought of leaving them was painful indeed. I was leaving, too, without the hope of ever being allowed to return. Master Thomas had said he would never let me return again. The barrier betwixt himself and brother he considered impassable.

I then had to regret that I did not at least make the attempt to carry out my resolution to run away; for the chances of success are tenfold greater from the city than from the country.

I sailed from Baltimore for St. Michael's in the sloop Amanda, Captain Edward Dodson. On my passage, I paid particular attention to the direction which the steamboats took to go to Philadelphia. I found, instead of going down, on reaching North Point they went up the bay, in a northeasterly direction. I deemed this knowledge of the utmost importance. My determination to run away was again revived. I resolved to wait only so long as the offering of a favorable opportunity. When that came, I was determined to be off.

CHAPTER IX

I HAVE now reached a period of my life when I can give dates. I left Baltimore, and went to live with Master Thomas Auld, at St. Michael's, in March, 1832. It was now more than seven years since I lived with him in the family of my old master, on Colonel Lloyd's plantation. We of course were now almost entire strangers to each other. He was to me a new master, and I to him a new slave. I was ignorant of his temper and disposition; he was equally so of mine. A very short time, however, brought us into full acquaintance with each other. I was made acquainted with his wife not less than with himself. They were well matched, being equally mean and cruel. I was now, for the first time during a space of more than seven years, made to feel the painful gnaw-ings of hunger— a something which I had not experienced before since I left Colonel Lloyd's plantation. It went hard enough with me then, when I could look back to no period at which I had enjoyed a sufficiency. It was tenfold harder after living in Master Hugh's family, where I had always had enough to eat, and of that which was good. I have said Mas-ter Thomas was a mean man. He was so. Not to give a slave enough to eat, is regarded as the most aggravated develop-ment of meanness even among slaveholders. The rule is, no matter how coarse the food, only let there be enough of it. This is the theory; and in the part of Maryland from which I came, it is the general practice,—though there are many exceptions. Master Thomas gave us enough of neither coarse nor fine food. There were four slaves of us in the kitchen— my sister Eliza, my aunt Priscilla, Henny, and myself; and we were allowed less than a half of a bushel of corn-meal per week, and very little else, either in the shape of meat or vegetables. It was not enough for us to subsist upon. We were therefore reduced to the wretched necessity of living at the expense of our neighbors. This we did by begging and stealing, whichever came handy in the time of need, the one being considered as legitimate as the other. A great many times have we poor creatures been nearly perishing with hunger, when food in abundance lay mouldering in the safe and smoke-house, and our pious mistress was aware of the fact; and yet that mistress and her husband would kneel every morning, and pray that God would bless them in basket and store!

Bad as all slaveholders are, we seldom meet one destitute of every element of character commanding respect. My master was one of this rare sort. I do not know of one single noble act ever performed by him. The leading trait in his character was meanness; and if there were any other element in his nature, it was made subject to this. He was mean; and, like most other mean men, he lacked the ability to conceal his meanness. Captain Auld was not born a slaveholder. He had been a poor man, master only of a Bay craft. He came into possession of all his slaves by marriage; and of all men, adopted slaveholders are the worst. He was cruel, but cowardly. He commanded without firmness. In the enforcement of his rules, he was at times rigid, and at times lax. At times, he spoke to his slaves with the firmness of Napoleon and the fury of a demon; at other times, he might well be mistaken for an inquirer who had lost his way. He did nothing of himself. He might have passed for a lion, but for his ears. In all things noble which he attempted, his own meanness shone most conspicuous. His airs, words, and actions, were the airs, words, and actions of born slaveholders, and, being assumed, were awkward enough. He was not even a good imitator. He possessed all the disposition to deceive, but wanted the power. Having no resources within himself, he was compelled to be the copyist of many, and being such, he was forever the victim of inconsistency; and of consequence he was an object of contempt, and was held as such even by his slaves. The luxury of having slaves of his own to wait upon him was something new and unprepared for. He was a slaveholder without the ability to hold slaves. He found himself incapable of managing his slaves either by force, fear, or fraud. We seldom called him "master;" we generally called him "Captain Auld," and were hardly disposed to title him at all. I doubt not that our conduct had much to do with making him appear awkward, and of consequence fretful. Our want of reverence for him must have perplexed him greatly. He wished to have us call him master, but lacked the firmness necessary to command us to do so. His wife used to insist upon our calling him so, but to no purpose. In August, 1832, my master attended a Methodist camp-meeting held in the Bay-side, Talbot county, and there experienced religion. I indulged a faint hope that his conversion would lead him to emancipate his slaves, and that, if he did not do this, it would, at any rate, make him more kind and humane. I was disappointed in both these respects. It neither made him to be humane to his slaves, nor to emancipate them. If it had any effect on his character, it made him more cruel and hateful in all his ways; for I believe him to have been a much worse man after his conversion than before. Prior to his conversion, he relied upon his own depravity to shield and sustain him in his savage barbarity; but after his conversion, he found religious sanction and support for his slaveholding cruelty. He made the greatest pretensions to piety. His house was the house of prayer. He prayed morning, noon, and night. He very soon distinguished himself among his brethren, and was soon made a class-leader and exhorter. His activity in revivals was great, and he proved himself an instrument in the hands of the church in converting many souls. His house was the preachers' home. They used to take great pleasure in coming there to put up; for while he starved us, he stuffed them. We have had three or four preachers there at a time. The names of those who used to come most frequently while I lived there, were Mr. Storks, Mr. Ewery, Mr. Humphry, and Mr. Hickey. I have also seen Mr. George Cookman at our house. We slaves loved Mr. Cookman. We believed him to be a good man. We thought him instrumental in getting Mr. Samuel Harrison, a very rich slaveholder, to emancipate his slaves; and by some means got the impression that he was laboring to effect the emancipation of all the slaves. When he was at our house, we were sure to be called in to prayers. When the others were there, we were sometimes called in and sometimes not. Mr. Cookman took more notice of us than either of the other ministers. He could not come among us without betraying his sympathy for us, and, stupid as we were, we had the sagacity to see it.

While I lived with my master in St. Michael's, there was a white young man, a Mr. Wilson, who proposed to keep a Sabbath school for the instruction of such slaves as might be disposed to learn to read the New Testament. We met but three times, when Mr. West and Mr. Fairbanks, both class-leaders, with many others, came upon us with sticks and other missiles, drove us off, and forbade us to meet again. Thus ended our little Sabbath school in the pious town of St. Michael's.

I have said my master found religious sanction for his cruelty. As an example, I will state one of many facts going to prove the charge. I have seen him tie up a lame young woman, and whip her with a heavy cowskin upon her naked shoulders, causing the warm red blood to drip; and, in justification of the bloody deed, he would quote this passage of Scripture—"He that knoweth his master's will, and doeth it not, shall be beaten with many stripes."

Master would keep this lacerated young, woman tied up in this horrid situation four or five hours at a time. I have known him to tie her up early in the morning, and whip her before breakfast; leave her, go to his store, return at dinner, and whip her again, cutting her in the places already made raw with his cruel lash. The secret of master's cruelty toward "Henny" is found in the fact of her being almost helpless. When quite a child, she fell into the fire, and burned herself horribly. Her hands were so burnt, that she never got the use of them. She could do very little but bear heavy burdens. She was to master a bill of expense; and as he was a mean man, she was a constant offence to him. He seemed desirous of getting the poor girl out of existence. He gave her away once to his sister; but, being a poor gift, she was not disposed to keep her. Finally, my benevolent master, to use his own words, "set her adrift to take care of herself." Here was a recently-converted man, holding on upon the mother, and at the same time turning out her helpless child, to starve and die! Master Thomas was one of the many pious slaveholders who hold slaves for the very charitable purpose of taking care of them.

My master and myself had quite a number of differences. He found me unsuitable to his purpose. My city life, he said, had had a very pernicious effect upon me. It had almost ruined me for every good purpose, and fitted me for every thing which was bad. One of my greatest faults was that of letting his horse run away, and go down to his father-in-law's farm, which was about five miles from St. Michael's. I would then have to go after it. My reason for this kind of carelessness, or carefulness, was, that I could always get something to eat when I went there. Master William Hamilton, my master's father-in-law, always gave his slaves enough to eat. I never left there hungry, no matter how great the need of my speedy return. Master Thomas at length said he would stand it no longer. I had lived with him nine months, during which time he had given me a number of severe whippings, all to no good purpose. He resolved to put me out, as he said, to be broken; and, for this purpose, he let me for one year to a man named Edward Covey. Mr. Covey was a poor man, a farm-renter. He rented the place upon which he lived, as also the hands with which he tilled it. Mr. Covey had acquired a very high reputation for breaking young slaves, and this reputation was of immense value to him. It enabled him to get his farm tilled with much less expense to himself than he could have had it done without such a reputation. Some slaveholders thought it not much loss to allow Mr. Covey to have their slaves one year, for the sake of the training to which they were subjected, without any other compensation. He could hire young help with great ease, in consequence of this reputation. Added to the natural good qualities of Mr. Covey, he was a professor of religion—a pious soul—a member and a class-leader in the Methodist church. All of this added weight to his reputation as a "nigger-breaker." I was aware of all the facts, having been made acquainted with them by a young man who had lived there. I nevertheless made the change gladly; for I was sure of getting enough to eat, which is not the smallest consideration to a hungry man.

CHAPTER X

I LEFT Master Thomas's house, and went to live with Mr. Covey, on the 1st of January, 1833. I was now, for the first time in my life, a field hand. In my new employment, I found myself even more awkward than a country boy appeared to be in a large city. I had been at my new home but one week before Mr. Covey gave me a very severe whipping, cutting my back, causing the blood to run, and raising ridges on my flesh as large as my little finger. The details of this affair are as follows: Mr. Covey sent me, very early in the morning of one of our coldest days in the month of January, to the woods, to get a load of wood. He gave me a team of unbroken oxen. He told me which was the in-hand ox, and which the off-hand one. He then tied the end of a large rope around the horns of the in-hand ox, and gave me the other end of it, and told me, if the oxen started to run, that I must hold on upon the rope. I had never driven oxen before, and of course I was very awkward. I, however, succeeded in getting to the edge of the woods with little difficulty; but I had got a very few rods into the woods, when the oxen took fright, and started full tilt, carrying the cart against trees, and over stumps, in the most frightful manner. I expected every moment that my brains would be dashed out against the trees.

After running thus for a considerable distance, they finally upset the cart, dashing it with great force against a tree, and threw themselves into it dense thicket. How I escaped death, I do not know. There I was, entirely alone, in a thick wood, in a place new to me. My cart was upset and shattered, my oxen were entangled among the young trees, and there was none to help me. After a long spell of effort, I succeeded in getting my cart righted, my oxen disentangled, and again yoked to the cart. I now proceeded with my team to the place where I had, the day before, been chopping wood, and loaded my cart pretty heavily, thinking in this way to tame my oxen. I then proceeded on my way home. I had now consumed one half of the day. I got out of the woods safely, and now felt out of danger, I stopped my oxen to open the woods gate; and just as I did so, before I could get hold of my ox-rope, the oxen again started, rushed through the gate, catching it between the wheel and the body of the cart, tearing it to pieces, and coming within a few inches of crushing me against the gate-post. Thus twice, in one short day, I escaped death by the merest chance. On my return, I told Mr. Covey what had happened, and how it happened. He ordered me to return to the woods again immediately. I did so, and he followed on after me. Just as I got into the woods, he came up and told me to stop my cart, and that he would teach me how to trifle away my time, and break gates. He then went to a large gum-tree, and with his axe cut three large switches, and, after trimming them up neatly with his pocket-knife, he ordered me to take off my clothes. I made him no answer, but stood with my clothes on. He repeated his order. I still made him no answer, nor did I move to strip myself. Upon this he rushed at me with the fierceness of a tiger, tore off my clothes, and lashed me till he had worn out his switches, cutting me so savagely as to leave the marks visible for a long time after. This whipping was the first of a number just like it, and for similar offences.

I lived with Mr. Covey one year. During the first six months, of that year, scarce a week passed without his whipping me. I was seldom free from a sore back. My awkwardness was almost always his excuse for whipping me. We were worked fully up to the point of endurance. Long before day we were up, our horses fed, and by the first approach of day we were off to the field with our hoes and ploughing teams. Mr. Covey gave us enough to eat, but scarce time to eat it. We were often less than five minutes taking our meals. We were often in the field from the first approach of day till its last lingering ray had left us; and at saving-fodder time, midnight often caught us in the field binding blades.

Covey would be out with us. The way he used to stand it, was this. He would spend the most of his afternoons in bed. He would then come out fresh in the evening, ready to urge us on with his words, example, and frequently with the whip. Mr. Covey was one of the few slaveholders who could and did work with his hands. He was a hard-working man. He knew by himself just what a man or a boy could do. There was no deceiving him. His work went on in his absence almost as well as in his presence; and he had the faculty of making us feel that he was ever present with us. This he did by surprising us. He seldom approached the spot where we were at work openly, if he could do it secretly. He always aimed at taking us by surprise. Such was his cunning, that we used to call him, among ourselves, "the snake." When we were at work in the cornfield, he would sometimes crawl on his hands and knees to avoid detection, and all at once he would rise nearly in our midst, and scream out, "Ha, ha! Come, come! Dash on, dash on!" This being his mode of attack, it was never safe to stop a single minute. His comings were like a thief in the night. He appeared to us as being ever at hand. He was under every tree, behind every stump, in every bush, and at every window, on the plantation. He would sometimes mount his horse, as if bound to St. Michael's, a distance of seven miles, and in half an hour afterwards you would see him coiled up in the corner of the wood-fence, watching every motion of the slaves. He would, for this purpose, leave his horse tied up in the woods. Again, he would sometimes walk up to us, and give us orders as though he was upon the point of starting on a long journey, turn his back upon us, and make as though he was going to the house to get ready; and, before he would get half way thither, he would turn short and crawl into a fence-corner, or behind some tree, and there watch us till the going down of the sun.

Mr. Covey's *forte* consisted in his power to deceive. His life was devoted to planning and perpetrating the grossest deceptions. Every thing he possessed in the shape of learning or religion, he made conform to his disposition to deceive. He seemed to think himself equal to deceiving the Almighty. He would make a short prayer in the morning, and a long prayer at night; and, strange as it may seem, few men would at times appear more devotional than he. The exercises of his family devotions were always commenced with singing; and, as he was a very poor singer himself, the duty of raising the hymn generally came upon me. He would read his hymn, and nod at me to commence. I would at times do so; at others, I would not. My non-compliance would almost always produce much confusion. To show himself independent of me, he would start and stagger through with his hymn in the most discordant manner. In this state of mind, he prayed with more than ordinary spirit. Poor man! Such was his disposition, and success at deceiving, I do verily believe that he sometimes deceived himself into the solemn belief, that he was a sincere worshipper of the most high God; and this, too, at a time when he may be said to have been guilty of compelling his woman slave to commit the sin of adultery. The facts in the case are these: Mr. Covey was a poor man; he was just commencing in life; he was only able to buy one slave; and, shocking as is the fact, he bought her, as he said, for a breeder. This woman was named Caroline. Mr. Covey bought her from Mr. Thomas Lowe, about six miles from

St. Michael's. She was a large, able-bodied woman, about twenty years old. She had already given birth to one child, which proved her to be just what he wanted. After buying her, he hired a married man of Mr. Samuel Harrison, to live with him one year; and him he used to fasten up with her every night! The result was, that, at the end of the year, the miserable woman gave birth to twins. At this result Mr. Covey seemed to be highly pleased, both with the man and the wretched woman. Such was his joy, and that of his wife, that nothing they could do for Caroline during her confinement was too good, or too hard, to be done. The children were regarded as being quite an addition to his wealth.

If at any one time of my life more than another, I was made to drink the bitterest dregs of slavery, that time was during the first six months of my stay with Mr. Covey. We were worked in all weathers. It was never too hot or too cold; it could never rain, blow, hail, or snow, too hard for us to work in the field. Work, work, work, was scarcely more the order of the day than of the night. The longest days were too short for him, and the shortest nights too long for him. I was somewhat unmanageable when I first went there, but a few months of this discipline tamed me. Mr. Covey succeeded in breaking me. I was broken in body, soul, and spirit. My natural elasticity was crushed, my intellect languished, the disposition to read departed, the cheerful spark that lingered about my eye died; the dark night of slavery closed in upon me; and behold a man transformed into a brute!

Sunday was my only leisure time. I spent this in a sort of beast-like stupor, between sleep and wake, under some large tree. At times I would rise up, a flash of energetic freedom would dart through my soul, accompanied with a faint beam of hope, that flickered for a moment, and then vanished. I sank down again, mourning over my wretched condition. I was sometimes prompted to take my life, and that of Covey, but was prevented by a combination of hope and fear. My sufferings on this plantation seem now like a dream rather than a stern reality.

Our house stood within a few rods of the Chesapeake Bay, whose broad bosom was ever white with sails from every quarter of the habitable globe. Those beautiful vessels, robed in purest white, so delightful to the eye of freemen, were to me so many shrouded ghosts, to terrify and torment me with thoughts of my wretched condition. I have often, in the deep stillness of a summer's Sabbath, stood all alone upon the lofty banks of that noble bay, and traced, with saddened heart and tearful eye, the countless number of sails moving off to the mighty ocean. The sight of these always affected me powerfully. My thoughts would compel utterance; and there, with no audience but the Almighty, I would pour out my soul's complaint, in my rude way, with an apostrophe to the moving multitude of ships:—

"You are loosed from your moorings, and are free; I am fast in my chains, and am a slave! You move merrily before the gentle gale, and I sadly before the bloody whip! You are freedom's swift-winged angels, that fly round the world; I am confined in bands of iron! O that I were free! O, that I were on one of your gallant decks, and under your protecting wing! Alas! betwixt me and you, the turbid waters roll. Go on, go on. O that I could also go! Could I but swim! If I could fly! O, why was I born a man, of whom to make a brute. The glad ship is gone; she hides in the dim distance. I am left in the hottest hell of unending slavery. O God, save me! God, deliver me! Let me be free! Is there any God? Why am I a slave? I will run away. I will not stand it. Get caught, or get clear, I'll try it. I had as well die with ague as the fever. I have only one life to lose. I had as well be killed running as die standing. Only think of it; one hundred miles straight north, and I am free! Try it? Yes! God helping me, I will. It cannot be that I shall live and die a slave. I will take to the water. This very bay shall yet bear me into freedom. The steamboats steered in a north-east course from North Point. I will do the same; and when I get to the head of the bay, I will turn my canoe adrift, and walk straight through Delaware into Pennsylvania. When I get there, I shall not be required to have a pass; I can travel without being disturbed. Let but the first opportunity offer, and, come what will, I am off. Meanwhile, I will try to bear up under the yoke. I am not the only slave in the world. Why should I fret? I can bear as much as any of them. Besides, I am but a boy, and all boys are bound to some one. It may be that my misery in slavery will only increase my happiness when I get free. There is a better day coming."

Thus I used to think, and thus I used to speak to myself; goaded almost to madness at one moment, and at the next reconciling myself to my wretched lot.

I have already intimated that my condition was much worse, during the first six months of my stay at Mr. Covey's, than in the last six. The circumstances leading to the change in Mr. Covey's course toward me form an epoch in my humble history. You have seen how a man was made a slave; you shall see how a slave was made a man. On one of the hottest days of the month of August, 1833, Bill Smith, William Hughes, a slave named Eli, and myself, were engaged in fanning wheat. Hughes was clearing the fanned wheat from before the fan, Eli was turning, Smith was feeding, and I was carrying wheat to the fan. The work was simple, requiring strength rather than intellect; yet, to one entirely unused to such work, it came very hard. About three o'clock of that day, I broke down; my strength failed me; I was seized with a violent aching of the head, attended with extreme dizziness; I trembled in every limb. Finding what was coming, I nerved myself up, feeling it would never do to stop work. I stood as long as I could stagger to the hopper with grain. When I could stand no longer, I fell, and felt as held down by an immense weight. The fan of course stopped; every one had his own work to do; and no one could do the work of the other, and have his own go on at the same time.

Mr. Covey was at the house, about one hundred yards from the treading-yard where we were fanning. On hearing the fan stop, he left immediately, and came to the spot where we were. He hastily inquired what the matter was. Bill answered that I was sick, and there was no one to bring wheat to the fan. I had by this time crawled away under the side of the post and rail-fence by which the yard was enclosed, hoping to find relief by getting out of the sun. He then asked where I was. He was told by one of the hands. He came to the spot, and, after looking at me awhile, asked me what was the matter. I told him as well as I could, for I scarce had strength to speak. He then gave me a savage kick in the side, and told me to get up. I tried to do so, but fell back in the attempt. He gave me another kick, and again told me to rise. I again tried, and succeeded in gaining my feet; but, stooping to get the tub with which I was feeding the fan, I again staggered and fell. While down in this situation, Mr. Covey took up the hickory slat with which Hughes had been striking off the half-bushel measure, and with it gave me a heavy blow upon the head, making a large wound, and the blood ran freely; and with this again told me to get up. I made no effort to comply, having now made up my mind to let him do his worst. In a short time after receiving this blow, my head grew better. Mr. Covey had now left me to my fate. At this moment I resolved, for the first time, to go to my master, enter a complaint, and ask his protection. In order to do this, I must that afternoon walk seven miles; and this, under the circumstances, was truly a severe undertaking. I was exceedingly feeble; made so as much by the kicks and blows which I received, as by the severe fit of sickness to which I had been subjected. I, however, watched my chance, while Covey was looking in an opposite direction, and started for St. Michael's. I succeeded in getting a considerable distance on my way to the woods, when Covey discovered me, and called after me to come back, threatening what he would do if I did not come. I, disregarded both his calls and his threats, and made my way to the woods as fast as my feeble state would allow; and thinking I might be overhauled by him if I kept the road, I walked through the woods, keeping far enough from the road to avoid detection, and near enough to prevent losing my way. I had not gone far before my little strength again failed me. I could go no farther. I fell down, and lay for a considerable time. The blood was yet oozing from the wound on my head. For a time I thought I should bleed to death; and think now that I should have done so, but that the blood so matted my hair as to stop the wound. After lying there about three quarters of an hour, I nerved myself up again, and started on my way, through bogs and briers, barefooted and bareheaded, tearing my feet sometimes at nearly every step; and after a journey of about seven miles, occupying some five hours to perform it, I arrived at master's store. I then presented an appearance enough to affect any but a heart of iron. From the crown of my head to my feet, I was covered with blood. My hair was all clotted with dust and blood; my shirt was stiff with blood. My legs and feet were torn in sundry places with briers and thorns, and were also covered with blood. I suppose I looked like a man who had escaped a den of wild beasts, and barely escaped them. In this state I appeared before my master, humbly entreating him to interpose his authority for my protection. I told him all the circumstances as well as I could, and it seemed, as I spoke, at times to affect him. He would then walk the floor, and seek to justify Covey by saying he expected I deserved it. He asked me what I wanted. I told him, to let me get a new home; that as sure as I lived with Mr. Covey again, I should live with but to die with him; that Covey would surely kill me; he was in a fair way for it. Master Thomas ridiculed the idea that there was any danger of Mr. Covey's killing me, and said that he knew Mr. Covey; that he was a good man, and that he could not think of taking me from him; that, should he do so, he would lose the whole year's wages; that I belonged to Mr. Covey for one year, and that I must go back to him, come what might; and that I must not trouble him with any more stories, or that he would himself *get hold of me*. After threatening me thus, he gave me a very large dose of salts, telling me that I might remain in St. Michael's that night, (it being quite late,) but that I must be off back to Mr. Covey's early in the morning; and that if I did not, he would *get hold of me*, which meant that he would whip me. I remained all night, and, according to his orders, I started off to Covey's in the morning,

(Saturday morning,) wearied in body and broken in spirit. I got no supper that night, or breakfast that morning. I reached Covey's about nine o'clock; and just as I was getting over the fence that divided Mrs. Kemp's fields from ours, out ran Covey with his cowskin, to give me another whipping. Before he could reach me, I succeeded in getting to the cornfield; and as the corn was very high, it afforded me the means of hiding. He seemed very angry, and searched for me a long time. My behavior was altogether unaccountable. He finally gave up the chase, thinking, I suppose, that I must come home for something to eat; he would give himself no further trouble in looking for me. I spent that day mostly in the woods, having the alternative before me,—to go home and be whipped to death, or stay in the woods and be starved to death. That night, I fell in with Sandy Jenkins, a slave with whom I was somewhat acquainted. Sandy had a free wife who lived about four miles from Mr. Covey's; and it being Saturday, he was on his way to see her. I told him my circumstances, and he very kindly invited me to go home with him. I went home with him, and talked this whole matter over, and got his advice as to what course it was best for me to pursue. I found Sandy an old adviser. He told me, with great solemnity, I must go back to Covey; but that before I went, I must go with him into another part of the woods, where there was a certain *root*, which, if I would take some of it with me, carrying it *always on my right side*, would render it impossible for Mr. Covey, or any other white man, to whip me. He said he had carried it for years; and since he had done so, he had never received a blow, and never expected to while he carried it. I at first rejected the idea, that the simple carrying of a root in my pocket would have any such effect as he had said, and was not disposed to take it; but Sandy impressed the necessity with much earnestness, telling me it could do no harm, if it did no good. To please him, I at length took the root, and, according to his direction, carried it upon my right side. This was Sunday morning. I immediately started for home; and upon entering the yard gate, out came Mr. Covey on his way to meeting. He spoke, to me very kindly, bade me drive the pigs from a lot near by, and passed on towards the church. Now, this singular conduct of Mr. Covey really made me begin to think that there was something in the *root* which Sandy, had given me; and had it been on any other day than Sunday, I could have attributed the conduct to no other cause than the influence of that root, and as it was, I was half inclined to think the *root* to be something more than I at first had taken it to be. All went well till Monday morning. On this morning, the virtue of the *root* was fully tested. Long before daylight I was called to go and rub, curry, and feed, the horses. I obeyed, and was glad to obey. But whilst thus engaged, whilst in the act of throwing down some blades from the loft, Mr. Covey entered the stable with a long rope; and just as I was half out of the loft, he caught hold of my legs, and was about tying me. As soon as I found what he was up to, I gave a sudden spring, and as I did so, he holding to my legs, I was brought sprawling on the stable floor. Mr. Covey seemed now to think he had me, and could do what he pleased; but at this moment—from whence came the spirit I don't know—I resolved to fight; and, suiting my action to the resolution, I seized Covey hard by the throat; and, as I did so, I rose. He held onto me, and I to him. My resistance was so entirely unexpected, that Covey seemed taken all aback. He trembled like a leaf. This gave me assurance, and I held him uneasy, causing the blood to run where I touched him with the ends of my fingers. Mr. Covey soon called out to Hughes for help. Hughes came, and, while Covey held me, attempted to tie my right hand. While he was in the act of doing so, I watched my chance, and gave him a heavy kick close under the ribs. This kick fairly sickened Hughes, so that he left me in the hands of Mr. Covey. This kick had the effect of not only weakening Hughes, but Covey also. When he saw Hughes bending over with pain, his courage quailed. He asked me if I meant to persist in my resistance. I told him I did, come what might; that he had used me like a brute for six months, and that I was determined to be used so no longer. With that, he strove to drag me to a stick that was lying just out of the stable door. He meant to knock me down. But just as he was leaning over to get the stick, I seized him with both hands by his collar, and brought him by a sudden snatch to the ground. By this time, Bill came. Covey called upon him for assistance. Bill wanted to know what he could do. Covey said, "Take hold of him, take hold of him!" Bill said his master hired him out to work, and not to help to whip me; so he left Covey and myself to fight our own battle out. We were at it for nearly two hours. Covey at length let me go, puffing and blowing at a great rate, saying that if I had not resisted, he would not have whipped me half so much. The truth was, that he had not whipped me at all. I considered him as getting entirely the worst end of the bargain; for he had drawn no blood from me, but I had from him. The whole six months afterwards, that I spent with Mr. Covey, he never laid the weight of his finger upon me in anger. He would occasionally say, he didn't want to get hold of me again. "No," thought I, "you need not; for you will come off worse than you did before."

This battle with Mr. Covey was the turning-point in my career as a slave. It rekindled the few expiring embers of freedom, and revived within me a sense of my own manhood. It recalled the departed self-confidence, and inspired me again with a determination to be free. The gratification afforded by the triumph was a full compensation for whatever else might follow, even death itself. He only can understand the deep satisfaction which I experienced, who has himself repelled by force the bloody arm of slavery. I felt as I never felt before. It was a glorious resurrection, from the tomb of slavery, to the heaven of freedom. My long-crushed spirit rose, cowardice departed, bold defiance took its place; and I now resolved that, however long I might remain a slave in form, the day had passed forever when I could be a slave in fact. I did not hesitate to let it be known of me, that the white man who expected to succeed in whipping, must also succeed in killing me.

From this time I was never again what might be called fairly whipped, though I remained a slave four years afterwards. I had several fights, but was never whipped.

It was for a long time a matter of surprise to me why Mr. Covey did not immediately have me taken by the constable to the whipping-post, and there regularly whipped for the crime of raising my hand against a white man in defence of myself. And the only explanation I can now think of does not entirely satisfy me; but such as it is, I will give it. Mr. Covey enjoyed the most unbounded reputation for being a first-rate overseer and negro-breaker. It was of considerable importance to him. That reputation was at stake; and had he sent me—a boy about sixteen years old—to the public whipping-post, his reputation would have been lost; so, to save his reputation, he suffered me to go unpunished.

My term of actual service to Mr. Edward Covey ended on Christmas day, 1833. The days between Christmas and New Year's day are allowed as holidays; and, accordingly, we were not required to perform any labor, more than to feed and take care of the stock. This time we regarded as our own, by the grace of our masters; and we therefore used or abused it nearly as we pleased. Those of us who had families at a distance, were generally allowed to spend the whole six days in their society. This time, however, was spent in various ways. The staid, sober, thinking and industrious ones of our number would employ themselves in making corn-brooms, mats, horse-collars, and baskets; and another class of us would spend the time in hunting opossums, hares, and coons. But by far the larger part engaged in such sports and merriments as playing ball, wrestling, running foot-races, fiddling, dancing, and drinking whisky; and this latter mode of spending the time was by far the most agreeable to the feelings of our masters. A slave who would work during the holidays was considered by our masters as scarcely deserving them. He was regarded as one who rejected the favor of his master. It was deemed a disgrace not to get drunk at Christmas; and he was regarded as lazy indeed, who had not provided himself with the necessary means, during the year, to get whisky enough to last him through Christmas.

From what I know of the effect of these holidays upon the slave, I believe them to be among the most effective means in the hands of the slaveholder in keeping down the spirit of insurrection. Were the slaveholders at once to abandon this practice, I have not the slightest doubt it would lead to an immediate insurrection among the slaves. These holidays serve as conductors, or safety-valves, to carry off the rebellious spirit of enslaved humanity. But for these, the slave would be forced up to the wildest desperation; and woe betide the slaveholder, the day he ventures to remove or hinder the operation of those conductors! I warn him that, in such an event, a spirit will go forth in their midst, more to be dreaded than the most appalling earthquake.

The holidays are part and parcel of the gross fraud, wrong, and inhumanity of slavery. They are professedly a custom established by the benevolence of the slaveholders; but I undertake to say, it is the result of selfishness, and one of the grossest frauds committed upon the down-trodden slave. They do not give the slaves this time because they would not like to have their work during its continuance, but because they know it would be unsafe to deprive them of it. This will be seen by the fact, that the slaveholders like to have their slaves spend those days just in such a manner as to make them as glad of their ending as of their beginning. Their object seems to be, to disgust their slaves with freedom, by plunging them into the lowest depths of dissipation. For instance, the slaveholders not only like to see the slave drink of his own accord, but will adopt various plans to make him drunk. One plan is, to make bets on their slaves, as to who can drink the most whisky without getting drunk; and in this way they succeed in getting whole multitudes to drink to excess. Thus, when the slave asks for virtuous freedom, the cunning slaveholder, knowing his ignorance, cheats him with a dose of vicious dissipation, artfully labelled with the name of liberty. The most of us used to drink it down, and the result was just what might be supposed: many of us were led to think that there was little to choose between liberty and slavery. We felt, and very properly too, that we had almost as well be slaves to man as to rum. So, when the holidays ended, we staggered up from the filth of our wallowing, took a long breath, and marched to the field,— feeling, upon the whole, rather glad to go, from what our master had deceived us into a belief was freedom, back to the arms of slavery.

I have said that this mode of treatment is a part of the whole system of fraud and inhumanity of slavery. It is so. The mode here adopted to disgust the slave with freedom, by allowing him to see only the abuse of it, is carried out in other things. For instance, a slave loves molasses; he steals some. His master, in many cases, goes off to town, and buys a large quantity; he returns, takes his whip, and commands the slave to eat the molasses, until the poor fellow is made sick at the very mention of it. The same mode is sometimes adopted to make the slaves refrain from asking for more food than their regular allowance. A slave runs through his allowance, and applies for more. His master is enraged at him; but, not willing to send him off without food, gives him more than is necessary, and compels him to eat it within a given time. Then, if he complains that he cannot eat it, he is said to be satisfied neither full nor fasting, and is whipped for being hard to please! I have an abundance of such illustrations of the same principle, drawn from my own observation, but think the cases I have cited sufficient. The practice is a very common one.

On the first of January, 1834, I left Mr. Covey, and went

to live with Mr. William Freeland, who lived about three miles from St. Michael's. I soon found Mr. Freeland a very different man from Mr. Covey. Though not rich, he was what would be called an educated southern gentleman. Mr. Covey, as I have shown, was a well-trained negro-breaker and slave-driver. The former (slaveholder though he was) seemed to possess some regard for honor, some reverence for justice and some respect for humanity. The latter seemed totally insensible to all such sentiments. Mr. Freeland had many of the faults peculiar to slaveholders, such as being very passionate and fretful; but I must do him the justice to say, that he was exceedingly free from those degrading vices to which Mr. Covey was constantly addicted. The one was open and frank, and we always knew where to find him. The other was a most artful deceiver, and could be understood only by such as were skilful enough to detect his cunningly-devised frauds. Another advantage I gained in my new master was, he made no pretensions to, or profession of, religion; and this, in my opinion, was truly a great advantage. I assert most unhesitatingly, that the religion of the south is a mere covering for the most horrid crimes, a justifier of the most appalling barbarity,—a sanctifier of the most hateful frauds,—and a dark shelter under, which the darkest, foulest, grossest, and most infernal deeds of slaveholders find the strongest protection. Were I to be again reduced to the chains of slavery, next to that enslavement, I should regard being the slave of a religious master the greatest calamity that could befall me. For of all slaveholders with whom I have ever met, religious slaveholders are the worst. I have ever found them the meanest and basest, the most cruel and cowardly, of all others. It was my unhappy lot not only to belong to a religious slaveholder, but to live in a community of such religionists. Very near Mr. Freeland lived the Rev. Daniel Weeden, and in the same neighborhood lived the Rev. Rigby Hopkins. These were members and ministers in the Reformed Methodist Church. Mr. Weeden owned, among others, a woman slave, whose name I have forgotten. This woman's back, for weeks, was kept literally raw, made so by the lash of this merciless, religious wretch. He used to hire hands. His maxim was, Behave well or behave ill, it is the duty of a master occasionally to whip a slave, to remind him of his master's authority. Such was his theory, and such his practice.

Mr. Hopkins was even worse than Mr. Weeden. His chief boast was his ability to manage slaves. The peculiar, feature of his government was that of whipping slaves in advance of deserving it. He always managed to have one or more of his slaves to whip every Monday morning. He did this to alarm their fears, and strike terror into those who escaped. His plan was to whip for the smallest offences, to prevent the commission of large ones. Mr. Hopkins could always find some excuse for whipping a slave. It would astonish one, unaccustomed to a slaveholding life, to see with what wonderful ease a slaveholder can find things, of which to make occasion to whip a slave. A mere look, word, or motion,—a mistake, accident, or want of power,—are all matters for which a slave may be whipped at any time. Does a slave look dissatisfied? It is said, he has the devil in him, and it must be whipped out. Does he speak loudly when spoken to by his master? Then he is getting high-minded, and should be taken down a button-hole lower. Does he forget to pull off his hat at the approach of a white person? Then he is want-ing in reverence, and should be whipped for it. Does he ever venture to vindicate his conduct, when censured for it? Then he is guilty of impudence,—one of the greatest crimes of which a slave can be guilty. Does he ever venture to suggest a different mode of doing things from that pointed out by his master? He is indeed presumptuous, and getting above himself; and nothing less than a flogging will do for him. Does he, while ploughing, break a plough,—or, while hoe-ing, break a hoe? It is owing to his carelessness, and for it a slave must always be whipped. Mr. Hopkins could always find something of this sort to justify the use of the lash, and he seldom failed to embrace such opportunities. There was not a man in the whole county, with whom the slaves who had the getting their own home, would not prefer to live, rather than with this Rev. Mr. Hopkins. And yet there was not a man any where round, who made higher professions of religion, or was more active in revivals,—more attentive to the class, love-feast, prayer and preaching meetings, or more devotional in his family,—that prayed earlier, later, louder, and longer,—than this same reverend slave-driver, Rigby Hopkins.

But to return to Mr. Freeland, and to my experience while in his employment. He, like Mr. Covey, gave us enough to eat; but, unlike Mr. Covey, he also gave us sufficient time to take our meals. He worked us hard, but always between sunrise and sunset. He required a good deal of work to be done, but gave us good tools with which to work. His farm was large, but he employed hands enough to work it, and with ease, compared with many of his neighbors. My treatment, while in his employment, was heavenly, compared with what I experienced at the hands of Mr. Edward Covey.

Mr. Freeland was himself the owner of but two slaves. Their names were Henry Harris and John Harris. The rest of his hands he hired. These consisted of myself, Sandy Jenkins,[53] and Handy Caldwell. Henry and John were quite intelligent, and in a very little while after I went there, I succeeded in creating in them a strong desire to learn how to read. This desire soon sprang up in the others also. They very soon mustered up some old spelling-books, and nothing would do but that I must keep a Sabbath school. I agreed to do so, and accordingly devoted my Sundays to teaching these my loved fellow-slaves how to read. Neither of them knew his letters when I went there. Some of the slaves of the neighboring farms found what was going on, and also availed themselves of this little opportunity to learn to read. It was understood, among all who came, that there must be as little display about it as possible. It was necessary to keep our religious masters at St. Michael's unacquainted with the fact, that, instead of spending the Sabbath in wrestling, boxing, and drinking whisky, we were trying to learn how to read the will of God; for they had much rather see us engaged in those degrading sports, than to see us behaving like intellectual, moral, and accountable beings. My blood boils as I think of the bloody manner in which Messrs. Wright Fairbanks and Garrison West, both class-leaders, in connection with many others, rushed in upon us with sticks and stones, and broke up our virtuous little Sabbath school, at St. Michael's—all calling themselves Christians! humble followers of the Lord Jesus Christ! But I am again digressing.

I held my Sabbath school at the house of a free colored man, whose name I deem it imprudent to mention; for should it be known, it might embarrass him greatly, though the crime of holding the school was committed ten years ago. I had at one time over forty scholars, and those of the right sort, ardently desiring to learn. They were of all ages, though mostly men and women. I look back to those Sundays with an amount of pleasure not to be expressed. They were great days to my soul. The work of instructing my dear fellow-slaves was the sweetest engagement with which I was ever blessed. We loved each other, and to leave them at the close of the Sabbath was a severe cross indeed. When I think that these precious souls are to-day shut up in the prison-house of slavery, my feelings overcome me, and I am almost ready to ask, "Does a righteous God govern the universe? and for what does he hold the thunders in his right hand, if not to smite the oppressor, and deliver the spoiled out of the hand of the spoiler?" These dear souls came not to Sabbath school because it was popular to do so, nor did I teach them because it was reputable to be thus engaged. Every moment they spent in that school, they were liable to be taken up, and given thirty-nine lashes. They came because they wished to learn. Their minds had been starved by their cruel masters. They had been shut up in mental darkness. I taught them, because it was the delight of my soul to be doing something that looked like bettering the condition of my race. I kept up my school nearly the whole year I lived with Mr. Freeland; and, beside my Sabbath school, I devoted three evenings in the week, during the winter, to teaching the slaves at home. And I have the happiness to know, that several of those who came to Sabbath school learned how to read; and that one, at least, is now free through my agency.

The year passed off smoothly. It seemed only about half as long as the year which preceded it. I went through it without receiving a single blow. I will give Mr. Freeland the credit of being the best master I ever had, *till I became my own master.* For the ease with which I passed the year, I was, however, somewhat indebted to the society of my fellow-slaves. They were noble souls; they not only possessed loving hearts, but brave ones. We were linked and inter-linked with each other. I loved them with a love stronger than any thing I have experienced since. It is sometimes said that we slaves do not love and confide in each other. In answer to this assertion, I can say, I never loved any or confided in any people more than my fellow-slaves, and especially those with whom I lived at Mr. Freeland's. I believe we would have died for each other. We never undertook to do any thing, of any importance, without a mutual consultation. We never moved separately. We were one; and as much so by our tempers and dispositions, as by the mutual hardships to which we were necessarily subjected by our condition as slaves.

At the close of the year 1834, Mr. Freeland again hired me of my master, for the year 1835. But, by this time, I began to want to live *upon free land* as well as *with Freeland*; and I was no longer content, therefore, to live with him or any other slaveholder. I began, with the commencement of the year, to prepare myself for a final struggle, which should decide my fate one way or the other. My tendency was upward. I was fast approaching manhood, and year after year had passed, and I was still a slave. These thought roused me—I must do something. I therefore resolved that 1835 should not pass without witnessing an attempt, on my part, to secure my liberty. But I was not willing to cherish this determination alone. My fellow-slaves were dear to me. I was anxious to have them participate with me in this, my life-giving determination. I therefore, though with great prudence, commenced early to ascertain their views and feelings in regard to their condition, and to imbue their minds with thoughts of freedom. I bent myself to devising ways and means for our escape, and meanwhile strove, on all fitting occasions, to impress them with the gross fraud and inhumanity of slavery. I went first to Henry, next to John, then to the others. I found, in them all, warm hearts and noble spirits. They were ready to hear, and ready to act when a feasible plan should be proposed. This was what I wanted. I talked to them of our want of manhood, if we submitted to our enslavement without at least one noble effort to be free. We met often, and consulted frequently, and told our hopes and fears, recounted the difficulties, real and imagined, which we should be called on to meet. At times we were almost disposed to give up, and try to content ourselves with our wretched lot; at others, we were firm and unbending in our determination to go. Whenever we suggested any plan, there was shrinking—the odds were fearful. Our path was beset with the greatest obstacles; and if we succeeded in gaining the end of it, our right to be free was yet questionable—we were yet liable to be returned to bondage. We could see no spot, this side of the ocean, where we could be free. We knew nothing about Canada. Our knowledge of the north did not extend farther than New York; and to go there, and be forever harassed with the frightful liability of being returned to slavery—with the certainty of being treated tenfold worse than before—the thought was truly a horrible one, and one which it was not easy to overcome. The case sometimes stood thus: At every gate through which we were to pass, we saw a watchman—at every ferry a guard—on every bridge a sentinel—and in every wood a patrol. We were hemmed in upon every side. Here were the difficulties, real or imagined—the good to be sought, and the evil to be shunned. On the one hand, there stood slavery, a stern reality, glaring frightfully upon us,—its robes already crimsoned with the blood of millions, and even now feasting itself greedily upon our own flesh. On the other hand, away back in the dim distance, under the flickering light of the north star, behind some craggy hill or snow-covered mountain, stood a doubtful freedom—half frozen—beckoning us to come and share its hospitality. This in itself was sometimes enough to stagger us; but when we permitted ourselves to survey the road, we were frequently appalled. Upon either side we saw grim death, assuming the most horrid shapes. Now it was starvation, causing us to eat our own flesh;—now we were contending with the waves, and were drowned;—now we were overtaken, and torn to pieces by the fangs of the terrible bloodhound. We were stung by scorpions, chased by wild beasts, bitten by snakes, and finally, after having nearly reached the desired spot,—after swimming rivers, encountering wild beasts, sleeping in the woods, suffering hunger and nakedness,—we were overtaken by our pursuers, and, in our resistance, we were shot dead upon the spot! I say, this picture sometimes appalled us, and made us

"rather bear those ills we had,
Than fly to others, that we knew not of."

In coming to a fixed determination to run away, we did more than Patrick Henry, when he resolved upon liberty or death. With us it was a doubtful liberty at most, and almost certain death if we failed. For my part, I should prefer death to hopeless bondage.

Sandy, one of our number, gave up the notion, but still encouraged us. Our company then consisted of Henry Harris, John Harris, Henry Bailey, Charles Roberts, and myself. Henry Bailey was my uncle, and belonged to my master. Charles married my aunt: he belonged to my master's father-in-law, Mr. William Hamilton.

The plan we finally concluded upon was, to get a large canoe belonging to Mr. Hamilton, and upon the Saturday night previous to Easter holidays, paddle directly up the Chesapeake Bay. On our arrival at the head of the bay, a distance of seventy or eighty miles from where we lived, it was our purpose to turn our canoe adrift, and follow the guidance of the north star till we got beyond the limits of Maryland. Our reason for taking the water route was, that we were less liable to be suspected as runaways; we hoped to be regarded as fishermen; whereas, if we should take the land route, we should be subjected to interruptions of almost every kind. Any one having a white face, and being so disposed, could stop us, and subject us to examination.

The week before our intended start, I wrote several protections, one for each of us. As well as I can remember, they were in the following words, to wit:—

"THIS is to certify that I, the undersigned, have given the bearer, my servant, full liberty to go to Baltimore, and spend the Easter holidays. Written with mine own hand, &c., 1835.

"WILLIAM HAMILTON,

"Near St. Michael's, in Talbot county, Maryland."

We were not going to Baltimore; but, in going up the bay, we went toward Baltimore, and these protections were only intended to protect us while on the bay.

As the time drew near for our departure, our anxiety became more and more intense. It was truly a matter of life and death with us. The strength of our determination was about to be fully tested. At this time, I was very active in explaining every difficulty, removing every doubt, dispelling every fear, and inspiring all with the firmness indispensable to success in our undertaking; assuring them that half was gained the instant we made the move; we had talked long enough; we were now ready to move; if not now, we never should be; and if we did not intend to move now, we had as well fold our arms, sit down, and acknowledge ourselves fit only to be slaves. This, none of us were prepared to acknowledge. Every man stood firm; and at our last meeting we pledged ourselves afresh, in the most solemn manner, that, at the time appointed, we would certainly start in pursuit of freedom. This was in the middle of the week, at the end of which we were to be off. We went, as usual, to our several fields of labor, but with bosoms highly agitated with thoughts of our truly hazardous undertaking. We tried to conceal our feelings as much as possible; and I think we succeeded very well.

After a painful waiting, the Saturday morning, whose night was to witness our departure, came. I hailed it with joy, bring what of sadness it might. Friday night was a sleepless one for me. I probably felt more anxious than the rest, because I was, by common consent, at the head of the whole affair. The responsibility of success or failure lay heavily upon me. The glory of the one, and the confusion of the other, were alike mine. The first two hours of that morning were such as I never experienced before, and hope never to again. Early in the morning, we went, as usual, to the field. We were spreading manure; and all at once, while thus engaged, I was overwhelmed with an indescribable feeling, in the fulness of which I turned to Sandy, who was near by, and said, "We are betrayed!" "Well," said he, "that thought has this moment struck me." We said no more. I was never more certain of any thing.

The horn was blown as usual, and we went up from the field to the house for breakfast. I went for the form, more than for want of any thing to eat that morning. Just as I got to the house, in looking, out at the lane gate, I saw four white men, with two colored men. The white men were on horseback, and the colored ones were walking behind, as if tied. I watched them a few moments till they got up to our lane gate. Here they halted, and tied the colored men to the gate-post. I was not yet certain as to what the matter was. In a few moments, in rode Mr. Hamilton, with a speed betokening great excitement. He came to the door, and inquired if Master William was in. He was told he was at the barn. Mr. Hamilton, without dismounting, rode up to the barn with extraordinary speed. In a few moments, he and Mr. Freeland returned to the house. By this time, the three constables rode up, and in great haste dismounted, tied their horses, and met Master William and Mr. Hamilton returning from the barn; and after talking awhile, they all walked up to the kitchen door. There was no one in the kitchen but myself and John. Henry and Sandy were up at the barn. Mr. Freeland put his head in at the door, and called me by name, saying, there were some gentlemen at the door who wished to see me. I stepped to the door, and inquired what they wanted. They at once seized me, and, without giving me any satisfaction, tied me—lashing my hands closely together. I insisted upon knowing what the matter was. They at length said, that they had learned I had been in a "scrape," and that I was to be examined before my master; and if their information proved false, I should not be hurt.

In a few moments, they succeeded in tying John. They then turned to Henry, who had by this time returned, and commanded him to cross his hands. "I won't!" said Henry, in a firm tone, indicating his readiness to meet the consequences of his refusal. "Won't you?" said Tom Graham, the constable. "No, I won't!" said Henry, in a still stronger tone. With this, two of the constables pulled out their shining pistols, and swore, by their Creator, that they would make him cross his hands or kill him. Each cocked his pistol, and, with fingers on the trigger, walked up to Henry, saying, at the same time, if he did not cross his hands, they would blow his damned heart out. "Shoot me, shoot me!" said Henry; "you can't kill me but once. Shoot, shoot,—and be damned! *I won't be tied!*" This he said in a tone of loud defiance; and at the same time, with a motion as quick as lightning, he with one single stroke dashed the pistols from the hand of each constable. As he did this, all hands fell upon him, and, after beating him some time, they finally overpowered him, and got him tied.

During the scuffle, I managed, I know not how, to get my pass out, and, without being discovered, put it into the fire. We were all now tied; and just as we were to leave for Easton jail, Betsy Freeland, mother of William Freeland, came to the door with her hands full of biscuits, and divided them between Henry and John. She then delivered herself of a speech, to the following effect:—addressing herself to me, she said, *"You devil! You yellow devil!* it was you that put it into the heads of Henry and John to run away. But for you, you long-legged mulatto devil! Henry nor John would never have thought of such a thing." I made no reply, and was immediately hurried off towards St. Michael's. Just a moment previous to the scuffle with Henry, Mr. Hamilton suggested the propriety of making a search for the protections which he had understood Frederick had written for himself and the rest. But, just at the moment he was about carrying his proposal into effect, his aid was needed in helping to tie Henry; and the excitement attending the scuffle caused them either to forget, or to deem it unsafe, under the circumstances, to search. So we were not yet convicted of the intention to run away.

When we got about half way to St. Michael's, while the constables having us in charge were looking ahead, Henry inquired of me what he should do with his pass. I told him to eat it with his biscuit, and own nothing; and we passed the word around, "Own nothing;" and "Own nothing!" said we all. Our confidence in each other was unshaken. We were resolved to succeed or fail together, after the calamity had befallen us as much as before. We were now prepared for any thing. We were to be dragged that morning fifteen miles behind horses, and then to be placed in the Easton jail. When we reached St. Michael's, we underwent a sort of examination. We all denied that we ever intended to run away. We did this more to bring out the evidence against us, than from any hope of getting clear of being sold; for, as I have said, we were ready for that. The fact was, we cared but little where we went, so we went together. Our greatest concern was about separation. We dreaded that more than any thing this side of death. We found the evidence against us to be the testimony of one person; our master would not tell who it was; but we came to a unanimous decision among ourselves as to who their informant was. We were sent off to the jail at Easton. When we got there, we were delivered up to the sheriff, Mr. Joseph Graham, and by him placed in jail. Henry, John, and myself, were placed in one room together—Charles, and Henry Bailey, in another. Their object in separating us was to hinder concert.

We had been in jail scarcely twenty minutes, when a swarm of slave traders, and agents for slave traders, flocked into jail to look at us, and to ascertain if we were for sale. Such a set of beings I never saw before! I felt myself surrounded by so many fiends from perdition. A band of pirates never looked more like their father, the devil. They laughed and grinned over us, saying, "Ah, my boys! we have got you, haven't we?" And after taunting us in various ways, they one by one went into an examination of us, with intent to ascertain our value. They would impudently ask us if we would not like to have them for our masters. We would make them no answer, and leave them to find out as best they could. Then they would curse and swear at us, telling us that they could take the devil out of us in a very little while, if we were only in their hands.

While in jail, we found ourselves in much more comfortable quarters, than we expected when we went there. We did not get much to eat, nor that which was very good;

but we had a good clean room, from the windows of which we could see what was going on in the street, which was very much better than though we had been placed in one of the dark, damp cells. Upon the whole, we got along very well, so far as the jail and its keeper were concerned. Immediately after the holidays were over, contrary to all our expectations, Mr. Hamilton and Mr. Freeland came up to Easton, and took Charles, the two Henrys, and John, out of jail, and carried them home, leaving me alone. I regarded this separation as a final one. It caused me more pain than any thing else in the whole transaction. I was ready for any thing rather than separation. I supposed that they had consulted together, and had decided that, as I was the whole cause of the intention of the others to run away, it was hard to make the innocent suffer with the guilty; and that they had, therefore, concluded to take the others home, and sell me, as a warning to the others that remained. It is due to the noble Henry to say, he seemed almost as reluctant at leaving the prison as at leaving home to come to the prison. But we knew we should, in all probability, be separated, if we were sold; and since he was in their hands, he concluded to go peaceably home.

I was now left to my fate. I was all alone, and within the walls of a stone prison. But a few days before, and I was full of hope. I expected to have been safe in a land of freedom; but now I was covered with gloom, sunk down to the utmost despair. I thought the possibility of freedom was gone.

I was kept in this way about one week, at the end of which, Captain Auld, my master, to my surprise and utter astonishment, came up, and took me out, with the intention of sending me, with a gentleman of his acquaintance, into Alabama. But, from some cause or other, he did not send me to Alabama, but concluded to send me back to Baltimore, to live again with his brother Hugh, and to learn a trade.

Thus, after an absence of three years and one month, I was once more permitted to return to my old home at Baltimore. My master sent me away, because there existed against me a very great prejudice in the community, and he feared I might be killed.

In a few weeks after I went to Baltimore, Master Hugh hired me to Mr. William Gardner, an extensive ship-builder, on Fell's Point. I was put there to learn how to calk. It, however, proved a very unfavorable place for the accomplishment of this object. Mr. Gardner was engaged that spring in building two large man-of-war brigs, professedly for the Mexican government. The vessels were to be launched in the July of that year, and in failure thereof, Mr. Gardner was to lose a considerable sum; so that when I entered, all was hurry. There was no time to learn any thing. Every man had to do that which he knew how to do. In entering the ship-yard, my orders from Mr. Gardner were, to do whatever the carpenters commanded me to do. This was placing me at the beck and call of about seventy-five men. I was to regard all these as masters. Their word was to be my law. My situation was a most trying one. At times I needed a dozen pair of hands. I was called a dozen ways in the space of a single minute. Three or four voices would strike my ear at the same moment. It was—"Fred., come help me to cant this timber here."—"Fred., come carry this timber yonder."—"Fred., bring that roller here."—"Fred., go get a fresh can of water."—"Fred., come help saw off the end of this timber."—"Fred., go quick, and get the crowbar."—"Fred., hold on the end of this fall."—"Fred., go to the blacksmith's shop, and get a new punch."—"Hurra, Fred.! run and bring me a cold chisel."—"I say, Fred., bear a hand, and get up a fire as quick as lightning under that steam-box."—"Halloo, nigger! come, turn this grindstone."—"Come, come! move, move! and bowse this timber forward."—"I say, darky, blast your eyes, why don't you heat up some pitch?"—"Halloo! halloo! halloo!" (Three voices at the same time.) "Come here!—Go there!—Hold on where you are! Damn you, if you move, I'll knock your brains out!"

This was my school for eight months; and I might have remained there longer, but for a most horrid fight I had with four of the white apprentices, in which my left eye was nearly knocked out, and I was horribly mangled in other respects. The facts in the case were these: Until a very little while after I went there, white and black ship-carpenters worked side by side, and no one seemed to see any impropriety in it. All hands seemed to be very well satisfied. Many of the black carpenters were freemen. Things seemed to be going on very well. All at once, the white carpenters knocked off, and said they would not work with free colored workmen. Their reason for this, as alleged, was, that if free colored carpenters were encouraged, they would soon take the trade into their own hands, and poor white men would be thrown out of employment. They therefore felt called upon at once to put a stop to it. And, taking advantage of Mr. Gardner's necessities, they broke off, swearing they would work no longer, unless he would discharge his black carpenters. Now, though this did not extend to me in form, it did reach me in fact. My fellow-apprentices very soon began to feel it degrading to them to work with me. They began to put on airs, and talk about the "niggers" taking the country, saying we all ought to be killed; and, being encouraged by the journeymen, they commenced making my condition as hard as they could, by hectoring me around, and sometimes striking me. I, of course, kept the vow I made after the fight with Mr. Covey, and struck back again, regardless of consequences; and while I kept them from combining, I succeeded very well; for I could whip the whole of them, taking them separately. They, however, at length combined, and came upon me, armed with sticks, stones, and heavy handspikes. One came in front with a half brick. There was one at each side of me, and one behind me. While I was attending to those in front, and on either side, the one behind ran up with the handspike, and struck me a heavy blow upon the head. It stunned me. I fell, and with this they all ran upon me, and fell to beating me with their fists. I let them lay on for a while, gathering strength. In an instant, I gave a sudden surge, and rose to my hands and knees. Just as I did that, one of their number gave me, with his heavy boot, a powerful kick in the left eye. My eyeball seemed to have burst. When they saw my eye closed, and badly swollen, they left me. With this I seized the handspike, and for a time pursued them. But here the carpenters interfered, and I thought I might as well give it up. It was impossible to stand my hand against so many. All this took place in sight of not less than fifty white ship-carpenters, and not one interposed a friendly word; but some cried, "Kill the damned nigger! Kill him! kill him! He struck a white person." I found my only chance for life was in flight. I succeeded in getting away without an additional blow, and barely so; for to strike a white man is death by Lynch law,—and that was the law in Mr. Gardner's ship-yard; nor is there much of any other out of Mr. Gardner's ship-yard.

I went directly home, and told the story of my wrongs to Master Hugh; and I am happy to say of him, irreligious as he was, his conduct was heavenly, compared with that of his brother Thomas under similar circumstances. He listened attentively to my narration of the circumstances leading to the savage outrage, and gave many proofs of his strong indignation at it. The heart of my once overkind mistress was again melted into pity. My puffed-out eye and blood-covered face moved her to tears. She took a chair by me, washed the blood from my face, and, with a mother's tenderness, bound up my head, covering the wounded eye with a lean piece of fresh beef. It was almost compensation for my suffering to witness, once more, a manifestation of kindness from this, my once affectionate old mistress. Master Hugh was very much enraged. He gave expression to his feelings by pouring out curses upon the heads of those who did the deed. As soon as I got a little the better of my bruises, he took me with him to Esquire Watson's, on Bond Street, to see what could be done about the matter. Mr. Watson inquired who saw the assault committed. Master Hugh told him it was done in Mr. Gardner's ship-yard, at midday, where there were a large company of men at work. "As to that," he said, "the deed was done, and there was no question as to who did it." His answer was, he could do nothing in the case, unless some white man would come forward and testify. He could issue no warrant on my word. If I had been killed in the presence of a thousand colored people, their testimony combined would have been insufficient to have arrested one of the murderers. Master Hugh, for once, was compelled to say this state of things was too bad. Of course, it was impossible to get any white man to volunteer his testimony in my behalf, and against the white young men. Even those who may have sympathized with me were not prepared to do this. It required a degree of courage unknown to them to do so; for just at that time, the slightest manifestation of humanity toward a colored person was denounced as abolitionism, and that name subjected its bearer to frightful liabilities. The watchwords of the bloody-minded in that region, and in those days, were, "Damn the abolitionists!" and "Damn the niggers!" There was nothing done, and probably nothing would have been done if I had been killed. Such was, and such remains, the state of things in the Christian city of Baltimore.

Master Hugh, finding he could get no redress, refused to let me go back again to Mr. Gardner. He kept me himself, and his wife dressed my wound till I was again restored to health. He then took me into the ship-yard of which he was foreman, in the employment of Mr. Walter Price. There I was immediately set to calking, and very soon learned the art of using my mallet and irons. In the course of one year from the time I left Mr. Gardner's, I was able to command the highest wages given to the most experienced calkers. I was now of some importance to my master. I was bringing him from six to seven dollars per week. I sometimes brought him nine dollars per week: my wages were a dollar and a half a day. After learning how to calk, I sought my own employment, made my own contracts, and collected the money which I earned. My pathway became much more smooth than before; my condition was now much more comfortable. When I could get no calking to do, I did nothing. During these leisure times, those old notions about freedom would steal over me again. When in Mr. Gardner's employment, I was kept in such a perpetual whirl of excitement, I could think of nothing, scarcely, but my life; and in thinking of my life, I almost forgot my liberty. I have observed this in my experience of slavery,—that whenever my condition was improved, instead of its increasing my contentment, it only increased my desire to be free, and set me to thinking of plans to gain my freedom. I have found that, to make a contented slave, it is necessary to make a thoughtless one. It is necessary to darken his moral and mental vision, and, as far as possible, to annihilate the power of reason. He must be able to detect no inconsistencies in slavery; he must be made to feel that slavery is right; and he can be brought to that only when be ceases to be a man.

I was now getting, as I have said, one dollar and fifty cents per day. I contracted for it; I earned it; it was paid to me; it was rightfully my own; yet, upon each returning Saturday night, I was compelled to deliver every cent of that money to Master Hugh. And why? Not because he earned it,—not because he had any hand in earning it,—not because I owed it to him,—nor because he possessed the slightest shadow of a right to it; but solely because he had the power to compel me to give it up. The right of the grim-visaged pirate upon the high seas is exactly the same.

CHAPTER XI

I NOW come to that part of my life during which I planned, and finally succeeded in making, my escape from slavery. But before narrating any of the peculiar circumstances, I deem it proper to make known my intention not to state all the facts connected with the transaction. My reasons for pursuing this course may be understood from the following: First, were I to give a minute statement of all the facts, it is not only possible, but quite probable, that others would thereby be involved in the most embarrassing difficulties. Secondly, such a statement would most undoubtedly induce greater vigilance on the part of slaveholders than has existed heretofore among them; which would, of course, be the means of guarding a door whereby some dear brother bondman might escape his galling chains. I deeply regret the necessity that impels me to suppress any thing of importance connected with my experience in slavery. It would afford me great pleasure indeed, as well as materially add to the interest of my narrative, were I at liberty to gratify a curiosity, which I know exists in the minds of many, by an accurate statement of all the facts pertaining to my most fortunate escape. But I must deprive myself of this pleasure, and the curious of the gratification which such a statement would afford. I would allow myself to suffer under the greatest imputations which evil-minded men might suggest, rather than exculpate myself, and thereby run the hazard of closing the slightest avenue by which a brother slave might clear himself of the chains and fetters of slavery.

I have never approved of the very public manner in which some of our western friends have conducted what they call the *underground railroad*, but which, I think, by their open declarations, has been made most emphatically the *upperground railroad*. I honor those good men and women for their noble daring, and applaud them for willingly subjecting themselves to bloody persecution, by openly avowing their participation in the escape of slaves. I, however, can see very little good resulting from such a course, either to themselves or the slaves escaping; while, upon the other hand, I see and feel assured that those open declarations are a positive evil to the slaves remaining, who are seeking to escape. They do nothing towards enlightening the slave, whilst they do much towards enlightening the master. They stimulate him to greater watchfulness, and enhance his power to capture his slave. We owe something to the slaves south of the line as well as to those north of it; and in aiding the latter on their way to freedom, we should be careful to do nothing which would be likely to hinder the former from escaping from slavery. I would keep the merciless slaveholder profoundly ignorant of the means of flight adopted by the slave. I would leave him to imagine himself surrounded by myriads of invisible tormentors, ever ready to snatch from his infernal grasp his trembling prey. Let him be left to feel his way in the dark; let darkness commensurate with his crime hover over him; and let him feel that at every step he takes, in pursuit of the flying bondman, he is running the frightful risk of having his hot brains dashed out by an invisible agency. Let us render the tyrant no aid; let us not hold the light by which he can trace the footprints of our flying brother. But enough of this, I will now proceed to the statement of those facts, connected with my escape, for which I am alone responsible, and for which no one can be made to suffer but myself.

In the early part of the year 1838, I became quite restless. I could see no reason why I should, at the end of each week, pour the reward of my toil into the purse of my master. When I carried to him my weekly wages, he would, after counting the money, look me in the face with a robber-like fierceness, and ask, "Is this all?" He was satisfied with nothing less than the last cent. He would, however, when I made him six dollars, sometimes give me six cents, to encourage me. It had the opposite effect. I regarded it as a sort of admission of my right to the whole. The fact that he gave me any part of my wages was proof, to my mind, that he believed me entitled to the whole of them. I always felt worse for having received any thing; for I feared that the giving me a few cents would ease his conscience, and make him feel himself to be a pretty honorable sort of robber. My discontent grew upon me. I was ever on the look-out for means of escape; and, finding no direct means, I determined to try to hire my time, with a view of getting money with which to make my escape. In the spring of 1838, when Master Thomas came to Baltimore to purchase his spring goods, I got an opportunity, and applied to him to allow me to hire my time. He unhesitatingly refused my request, and told me this was another stratagem by which to escape. He told me I could go nowhere but that he could get me; and that, in the event of my running away, he should spare no pains in his efforts to catch me. He exhorted me to content myself, and be obedient. He told me, if I would be happy, I must lay out no plans for the future. He said, if I behaved myself properly, he would take care of me. Indeed, he advised me to complete thoughtlessness of the future, and taught me to depend solely upon him for happiness. He seemed to see fully the pressing necessity of setting aside my intellectual nature, in order to contentment in slavery. But in spite of him, and even in spite of myself, I continued to think, and to think about the injustice of my enslavement, and the means of escape.

About two months after this, I applied to Master Hugh for the privilege of hiring my time. He was not acquainted with the fact that I had applied to Master Thomas, and had been refused. He too, at first, seemed disposed to refuse; but, after some reflection, he granted me the privilege, and proposed the following terms: I was to be allowed all my time, make all contracts with those for whom I worked,

and find my own employment; and, in return for this liberty, I was to pay him three dollars at the end of each week;
find myself in calking tools, and in board and clothing. My
board was two dollars and a half per week. This, with the
wear and tear of clothing and calking tools, made my regular expenses about six dollars per week. This amount I was
compelled to make up, or relinquish the privilege of hiring
my time. Rain or shine, work or no work, at the end of
each week the money must be forthcoming, or I must give
up my privilege. This arrangement, it will be perceived, was
decidedly in my master's favor. It relieved him of all need of
looking after me. His money was sure. He received all the
benefits of slaveholding without its evils; while I endured
all the evils of a slave, and suffered all the care and anxiety
of a freeman. I found it a hard bargain. But, hard as it was,
I thought it better than the old mode of getting along. It
was a step towards freedom to be allowed to bear the responsibilities of a freeman, and I was determined to hold
on upon it. I bent myself to the work of making money. I
was ready to work at night as well as day, and by the most
untiring perseverance and industry, I made enough to meet
my expenses, and lay up a little money every week. I went
on thus from May till August. Master Hugh then refused
to allow me to hire my time longer. The ground for his refusal was a failure on my part, one Saturday night, to pay
him for my week's time. This failure was occasioned by my
attending a camp meeting about ten miles from Baltimore.

During the week, I had entered into an engagement with a number of young friends to start from Baltimore to the camp ground early Saturday evening; and being detained by my employer, I was unable to get down to Master Hugh's without disappointing the company. I knew that Master Hugh was in no special need of the money that night. I therefore decided to go to camp meeting, and upon my return pay him the three dollars. I staid at the camp meeting one day longer than I intended when I left. But as soon as I returned, I called upon him to pay him what he considered his due. I found him very angry; he could scarce restrain his wrath. He said he had a great mind to give me a severe whipping. He wished to know how I dared go out of the city without asking his permission. I told him I hired my time, and while I paid him the price which he asked for it, I did not know that I was bound to ask him when and where I should go. This reply troubled him; and, after reflecting a few moments, he turned to me, and said I should hire my time no longer; that the next thing he should know of, I would be running away. Upon the same plea, he told me to bring my tools and clothing home forthwith. I did so; but instead of seeking work, as I had been accustomed to do previously to hiring my time, I spent the whole week without the performance of a single stroke of work. I did this in retaliation. Saturday night, he called upon me as usual for my week's wages. I told him I had no wages; I had done no work that week. Here we were upon the point of coming to blows. He raved, and swore his determination to get hold of me. I did not allow myself a single word; but was resolved, if he laid the weight of his hand upon me, it should be blow for blow. He did not strike me, but told me that he would find me in constant employment in future. I thought the matter over during the next day, Sunday, and finally resolved upon the third day of September, as the day upon which I would make a second attempt to secure my freedom. I now had three weeks during which to prepare for my journey. Early on Monday morning, before Master Hugh had time to make any engagement for me, I went out and got employment of Mr. Butler, at his ship-yard near the drawbridge, upon what is called the City Block, thus making it unnecessary for him to seek employment for me. At the end of the week, I brought him between eight and nine dollars. He seemed very well pleased, and asked me why I did not do the same the week before. He little knew what my plans were. My object in working steadily was to remove any suspicion he might entertain of my intent to run away; and in this I succeeded admirably. I suppose he thought I was never better satisfied with my condition than at the very time during which I was planning my escape. The second week passed, and again I carried him my full wages; and so well pleased was he, that he gave me twenty-five cents, (quite a large sum for a slaveholder to give a slave,) and bade me to make a good use of it. I told him I would.

Things went on without very smoothly indeed, but within there was trouble. It is impossible for me to describe my feelings as the time of my contemplated start drew near. I had a number of warm-hearted friends in Baltimore,—friends that I loved almost as I did my life,—and the thought of being separated from them forever was painful beyond expression. It is my opinion that thousands would escape from slavery, who now remain, but for the strong cords of affection that bind them to their friends. The thought of leaving my friends was decidedly the most painful thought with which I had to contend. The love of them was my tender point, and shook my decision more than all things else. Besides the pain of separation, the dread and apprehension of a failure exceeded what I had experienced at my first attempt. The appalling defeat I then sustained returned to torment me. I felt assured that, if I failed in this attempt, my case would be a hopeless one—it would seat my fate as a slave forever. I could not hope to get off with any thing less than the severest punishment, and being placed beyond the means of escape. It required no very vivid imagination to depict the most frightful scenes through which I should have to pass, in case I failed. The wretchedness of slavery, and the blessedness of freedom, were perpetually before me. It was life and death with me. But I remained firm, and, according to my resolution, on the third day of September, 1838, I left my chains, and succeeded in reaching New York without the slightest interruption of any kind. How I did so,—what means I adopted,—what direction I travelled, and by what mode of conveyance,—I must leave unexplained, for the reasons before mentioned.

I have been frequently asked how I felt when I found myself in a free State. I have never been able to answer the question with any satisfaction to myself. It was a moment of the highest excitement I ever experienced. I suppose I felt as one may imagine the unarmed mariner to feel when he is rescued by a friendly man-of-war from the pursuit of a pirate. In writing to a dear friend, immediately after my arrival at New York, I said I felt like one who had escaped a den of hungry lions. This state of mind, however, very soon subsided; and I was again seized with a feeling of great insecurity and loneliness. I was yet liable to be taken back, and subjected to all the tortures of slavery. This in itself was enough to damp the ardor of my enthusiasm. But the loneliness overcame me. There I was in the midst of thousands, and yet a perfect stranger; without home and without friends, in the midst of thousands of my own brethren—children of a common Father, and yet I dared not to unfold to any one of them my sad condition. I was afraid to speak to any one for fear of speaking to the wrong one, and thereby falling into the hands of money-loving kidnappers, whose business it was to lie in wait for the panting fugitive, as the ferocious beasts of the forest lie in wait for their prey. The motto which I adopted when I started from slavery was this—"Trust no man!" I saw in every white man an enemy, and in almost every colored man cause for distrust. It was a most painful situation; and, to understand it, one must needs experience it, or imagine himself in similar circumstances. Let him be a fugitive slave in a strange land—a land given up to be the hunting-ground for slaveholders—whose inhabitants are legalized kidnappers—where he is every moment subjected to the terrible liability of being seized upon by his fellowmen, as the hideous crocodile seizes upon his prey!—say, let him place himself in my situation—without home or friends—without money or credit—wanting shelter, and no one to give it—wanting bread, and no money to buy it,—and at the same time let him feel that he is pursued by merciless men-hunters, and in total darkness as to what to do, where to go, or where to stay,—perfectly helpless both as to the means of defence and means of escape,—in the midst of plenty, yet suffering the terrible gnawings of hunger,—in the midst of houses, yet having no home,—among fellow-men, yet feeling as if in the midst of wild beasts, whose greediness to swallow up the trembling and half-famished fugitive is only equalled by that with which the monsters of the deep swallow up the helpless fish upon which they subsist,—I say, let him be placed in this most trying situation,—the situation in which I was placed,—then, and not till then, will he fully appreciate the hardships of, and know how to sympathize with, the toil-worn and whip-scarred fugitive slave.

Thank Heaven, I remained but a short time in this distressed situation. I was relieved from it by the humane hand of Mr. DAVID RUGGLES, whose vigilance, kindness, and per-severance, I shall never forget. I am glad of an opportunity to express, as far as words can, the love and gratitude I bear him. Mr. Ruggles is now afflicted with blindness, and is himself in need of the same kind offices which he was once so forward in the performance of toward others. I had been in New York but a few days, when Mr. Ruggles sought me out, and very kindly took me to his boarding-house at the corner of Church and Lespenard Streets. Mr. Ruggles was then very deeply engaged in the memorable Darg case, as well as attending to a number of other fugitive slaves, devising ways and means for their successful escape; and, though watched and hemmed in on almost every side, he seemed to be more than a match for his enemies.

Very soon after I went to Mr. Ruggles, he wished to know of me where I wanted to go; as he deemed it unsafe for me to remain in New York. I told him I was a calker, and should like to go where I could get work. I thought of going to Canada; but he decided against it, and in favor of my going to New Bedford, thinking I should be able to get work there at my trade. At this time, Anna,[54] my intended wife, came on; for I wrote to her immediately after my arrival at New York, (notwithstanding my homeless, houseless, and helpless condition,) informing her of my successful flight, and wishing her to come on forthwith. In a few days after her arrival, Mr. Ruggles called in the Rev. J. W. C. Pennington, who, in the presence of Mr. Ruggles, Mrs.

Michaels, and two or three others, performed the marriage ceremony, and gave us a certificate, of which the following is an exact copy:—

"This may certify, that I joined together in holy matrimony Frederick Johnson[55] and Anna Murray, as man and wife, in the presence of Mr. David Ruggles and Mrs. Michaels.

"JAMES W. C. PENNINGTON.

"*New York, Sept. 15, 1838.*"

Upon receiving this certificate, and a five-dollar bill from Mr. Ruggles, I shouldered one part of our baggage, and Anna took up the other, and we set out forthwith to take passage on board of the steamboat John W. Richmond for Newport, on our way to New Bedford. Mr. Ruggles gave me a letter to a Mr. Shaw in Newport, and told me, in case my money did not serve me to New Bedford, to stop in Newport and obtain further assistance; but upon our arrival at Newport, we were so anxious to get to a place of safety, that, notwithstanding we lacked the necessary money to pay our fare, we decided to take seats in the stage, and promise to pay when we got to New Bedford. We were encouraged to do this by two excellent gentlemen, residents of New Bedford, whose names I afterward ascertained to be Joseph Ricketson and William C. Taber. They seemed at once to understand our circumstances, and gave us such assurance of their friendliness as put us fully at ease in their presence. It was good indeed to meet with such friends, at such a time. Upon reaching New Bedford, we were directed to the house of Mr. Nathan Johnson, by whom we were kindly received, and hospitably provided for. Both Mr. and Mrs. Johnson took a deep and lively interest in our welfare. They proved themselves quite worthy of the name of abolitionists. When the stage-driver found us unable to pay our fare, he held on upon our baggage as security for the debt. I had but to mention the fact to Mr. Johnson, and he forthwith advanced the money.

We now began to feel a degree of safety, and to prepare ourselves for the duties and responsibilities of a life of freedom. On the morning after our arrival at New Bedford, while at the breakfast-table, the question arose as to what name I should be called by. The name given me by my mother was, "Frederick Augustus Washington Bailey." I, however, had dispensed with the two middle names long before I left Maryland, so that I was generally known by the name of "Frederick Bailey." I started from Baltimore bearing the name of "Stanley." When I got to New York, I again changed my name to "Frederick Johnson," and thought that would be the last change. But when I got to New Bedford, I found it necessary again to change my name. The reason of this necessity was, that there were so many Johnsons in New Bedford, it was already quite difficult to distinguish between them. I gave Mr. Johnson the privilege of choosing me a name, but told him be must not take from me the name of "Frederick." I must hold on to that, to preserve a sense of my identity. Mr. Johnson had just been reading the "Lady of the Lake," and at once suggested that my name be "Douglass." From that time until now I have been called "Frederick Douglass;" and as I am more widely known by that name than by either of the others, I shall continue to use it as my own.

I was quite disappointed at the general appearance of things in New Bedford. The impression which I had received respecting the character and condition of the people of the north, I found to be singularly erroneous. I had very strangely supposed, while in slavery, that few of the comforts, and scarcely any of the luxuries, of life were enjoyed at the north, compared with what were enjoyed by the slaveholders of the south. I probably came to this conclusion from the fact that northern people owned no slaves. I supposed that they were about upon a level with the non-slaveholding population of the south. I knew they were exceedingly poor, and I had been accustomed to regard their poverty as the necessary consequence of their being non-slaveholders. I had somehow imbibed the opinion that, in the absence of slaves, there could be no wealth, and very little refinement. And upon coming to the north, I expected to meet with a rough, hard-handed, and uncultivated population, living in the most Spartan-like simplicity, knowing nothing of the ease, luxury, pomp, and grandeur of southern slaveholders. Such being my conjectures, any one acquainted with the appearance of New Bedford may very readily infer how palpably I must have seen my mistake.

In the afternoon of the day when I reached New Bedford, I visited the wharves, to take a view of the shipping. Here I found myself surrounded with the strongest proofs of wealth. Lying at the wharves, and riding in the stream, I saw many ships of the finest model, in the best order, and of the largest size. Upon the right and left, I was walled in by granite warehouses of the widest dimensions, stowed to their utmost capacity with the necessaries and comforts of life. Added to this, almost every body seemed to be at work, but noiselessly so, compared with what I had been accustomed to in Baltimore. There were no loud songs heard from those engaged in loading and unloading ships. I heard no deep oaths or horrid curses on the laborer. I saw no whipping of men; but all seemed to go smoothly on. Every man appeared to understand his work, and went at it with a sober, yet cheerful earnestness, which betokened the deep interest which he felt in what he was doing, as well as a sense of his own dignity as a man. To me this looked exceedingly strange. From the wharves I strolled around and over the town, gazing with wonder and admiration at the splendid churches, beautiful dwellings, and finely-cultivated gardens; evincing an amount of wealth, comfort, taste, and refinement, such as I had never seen in any part of slaveholding Maryland.

Every thing looked clean, new, and beautiful. I saw few or no dilapidated houses, with poverty-stricken inmates;

no half-naked children and barefooted women, such as I had been accustomed to see in Hillsborough, Easton, St. Michael's, and Baltimore. The people looked more able, stronger, healthier, and happier, than those of Maryland. I was for once made glad by a view of extreme wealth, without being saddened by seeing extreme poverty. But the most astonishing as well as the most interesting thing to me was the condition of the colored people, a great many of whom, like myself, had escaped thither as a refuge from the hunters of men. I found many, who had not been seven years out of their chains, living in finer houses, and evidently enjoying more of the comforts of life, than the average of slaveholders in Maryland. I will venture to assert that my friend Mr. Nathan Johnson (of whom I can say with a grateful heart, "I was hungry, and he gave me meat; I was thirsty, and he gave me drink; I was a stranger, and he took me in") lived in a neater house; dined at a better table; took, paid for, and read, more newspapers; better understood the moral, religious, and political character of the nation,—than nine tenths of the slaveholders in Talbot county, Maryland. Yet Mr. Johnson was a working man. His hands were hardened by toil, and not his alone, but those also of Mrs. Johnson. I found the colored people much more spirited than I had supposed they would be. I found among them a determination to protect each other from the blood-thirsty kidnapper, at all hazards. Soon after my arrival, I was told of a circumstance which illustrated their spirit. A colored man and a fugitive slave were on unfriendly terms. The former was heard to threaten the latter with informing his master of his whereabouts. Straightway a meeting was called among the colored people, under the stereotyped notice, "Business of importance!" The betrayer was invited to attend. The people came at the appointed hour, and organized the meeting by appointing a very religious old gentleman as president, who, I believe, made a prayer, after which he addressed the meeting as follows: *"Friends, we have got him here, and I would recommend that you young men just take him outside the door, and kill him!"* With this, a number of them bolted at him; but they were intercepted by some more timid than themselves, and the betrayer escaped their vengeance, and has not been seen in New Bedford since. I believe there have been no more such threats, and should there be hereafter, I doubt not that death would be the consequence.

I found employment, the third day after my arrival, in stowing a sloop with a load of oil. It was new, dirty, and hard work for me; but I went at it with a glad heart and a willing hand. I was now my own master. It was a happy moment, the rapture of which can be understood only by those who have been slaves. It was the first work, the reward of which was to be entirely my own. There was no Master Hugh standing ready, the moment I earned the money, to rob me of it. I worked that day with a pleasure I had never before experienced. I was at work for myself and newly-married wife. It was to me the starting-point of a new existence. When I got through with that job, I went in pursuit of a job of calking; but such was the strength of prejudice against color, among the white calkers, that they refused to work with me, and of course I could get no employment.[56] Finding my trade of no immediate benefit, I threw off my calking habiliments, and prepared myself to do any kind of work I could get to do. Mr. Johnson kindly let me have his wood-horse and saw, and I very soon found myself a plenty of work. There was no work too hard—none too dirty. I was ready to saw wood, shovel coal, carry the hod, sweep the chimney, or roll oil casks,—all of which I did for nearly three years in New Bedford, before I became known to the anti-slavery world.

In about four months after I went to New Bedford, there came a young man to me, and inquired if I did not wish to take the "Liberator." I told him I did; but, just having made my escape from slavery, I remarked that I was unable to pay for it then. I, however, finally became a subscriber to it. The paper came, and I read it from week to week with such feelings as it would be quite idle for me to attempt to describe. The paper became my meat and my drink. My soul was set all on fire. Its sympathy for my brethren in bonds—its scathing denunciations of slaveholders—its faithful exposures of slavery—and its powerful attacks upon the upholders of the institution—sent a thrill of joy through my soul, such as I had never felt before!

I had not long been a reader of the "Liberator," before I got a pretty correct idea of the principles, measures and spirit of the anti-slavery reform. I took right hold of the cause. I could do but little; but what I could, I did with a joyful heart, and never felt happier than when in an anti-slavery meeting. I seldom had much to say at the meetings, because what I wanted to say was said so much better by others. But, while attending an anti-slavery convention at Nantucket, on the 11th of August, 1841, I felt strongly moved to speak, and was at the same time much urged to do so by Mr. William C. Coffin, a gentleman who had heard me speak in the colored people's meeting at New Bedford. It was a severe cross, and I took it up reluctantly. The truth was, I felt myself a slave, and the idea of speaking to white people weighed me down. I spoke but a few moments, when I felt a degree of freedom, and said what I desired with considerable ease. From that time until now, I have been engaged in pleading the cause of my brethren—with what success, and with what devotion, I leave those acquainted with my labors to decide.

APPENDIX

I FIND, since reading over the foregoing Narrative that I have, in several instances, spoken in such a tone and manner, respecting religion, as may possibly lead those unacquainted with my religious views to suppose me an opponent of all religion. To remove the liability of such misapprehension, I deem it proper to append the following brief explanation. What I have said respecting and against religion, I mean strictly to apply to the *slaveholding religion* of this land, and with no possible reference to Christianity proper; for, between the Christianity of this land, and the Christianity of Christ, I recognize the widest possible difference—so wide, that to receive the one as good, pure, and holy, is of necessity to reject the other as bad, corrupt, and wicked. To be the friend of the one, is of necessity to be the enemy of the other. I love the pure, peaceable, and impartial Christianity of Christ: I therefore hate the corrupt, slaveholding, women-whipping, cradle-plundering, partial and hypocritical Christianity of this land. Indeed, I can see no reason, but the most deceitful one, for calling the religion of this land Christianity. I look upon it as the climax of all misnomers, the boldest of all frauds, and the grossest of all libels. Never was there a clearer case of "stealing the

237

livery of the court of heaven to serve the devil in." I am filled with unutterable loathing when I contemplate the religious pomp and show, together with the horrible inconsistencies, which every where surround me. We have men-stealers for ministers, women-whippers for missionaries, and cradle-plunderers for church members. The man who wields the blood-clotted cowskin during the week fills the pulpit on Sunday, and claims to be a minister of the meek and lowly Jesus. The man who robs me of my earnings at the end of each week meets me as a class-leader on Sunday morning, to show me the way of life, and the path of salvation. He who sells my sister, for purposes of prostitution, stands forth as the pious advocate of purity. He who proclaims it a religious duty to read the Bible denies me the right of learning to read the name of the God who made me. He who is the religious advocate of marriage robs whole millions of its sacred in-fluence, and leaves them to the ravages of wholesale pol-lution. The warm defender of the sacredness of the family relation is the same that scatters whole families,—sunder-ing husbands and wives, parents and children, sisters and brothers, leaving the hut vacant, and the hearth desolate. We see the thief preaching against theft, and the adulter-er against adultery. We have men sold to build churches, women sold to support the gospel, and babes sold to pur-chase Bibles for the *poor heathen! all for the glory of God and the good of souls!* The slave auctioneer's bell and the church-going bell chime in with each other, and the bitter cries of the heart-broken slave are drowned in the religious shouts of his pious master. Revivals of religion and revivals in the slave-trade go hand in hand together. The slave prison and the church stand near each other. The clanking of fetters and the rattling of chains in the prison, and the pious psalm and solemn prayer in the church, may be heard at the same time. The dealers in the bodies and souls of men erect their stand in the presence of the pulpit, and they mutually help each other. The dealer gives his blood-stained gold to support the pulpit, and the pulpit, in return, covers his infernal business with the garb of Christianity. Here we have religion and robbery the allies of each other—devils dressed in angels' robes, and hell presenting the semblance of paradise.

> "Just God! and these are they,
>   Who minister at thine altar, God of right!
> Men who their hands, with prayer and blessing, lay
>   On Israel's ark of light.
>
> "What! preach, and kidnap men?
>   Give thanks, and rob thy own afflicted poor?
> Talk of thy glorious liberty, and then
>   Bolt hard the captive's door?
>
> "What! servants of thy own
>   Merciful Son, who came to seek and save
> The homeless and the outcast, fettering down
>   The tasked and plundered slave!
>
> "Pilate and Herod friends!
>   Chief priests and rulers, as of old, combine!

Just God and holy! is that church which lends
        Strength to the spoiler thine?"

The Christianity of America is a Christianity, of whose votaries it may be as truly said, as it was of the ancient scribes and Pharisees, "They bind heavy burdens, and grievous to be borne, and lay them on men's shoulders, but they themselves will not move them with one of their fingers. All their works they do for to be seen of men.—They love the uppermost rooms at feasts, and the chief seats in the synagogues, . . . and to be called of men, Rabbi, Rabbi.—But woe unto you, scribes and Pharisees, hypocrites! for ye shut up the kingdom of heaven against men; for ye neither go in yourselves, neither suffer ye them that are entering to go in. Ye devour widows' houses, and for a pretence make long prayers; therefore ye shall receive the greater damnation. Ye compass sea and land to make one proselyte, and when he is made, ye make him twofold more the child of hell than yourselves.—Woe unto you, scribes and Pharisees, hypocrites! for ye pay tithe of mint, and anise, and cumin, and have omitted the weightier matters of the law, judgment, mercy, and faith; these ought ye to have done, and not to leave the other undone. Ye blind guides! which strain at a gnat, and swallow a camel. Woe unto you, scribes and Pharisees, hypocrites! for ye make clean the outside of the cup and of the platter; but within, they are full of extortion and excess.—Woe unto you, scribes and Pharisees, hypocrites!

for ye are like unto whited sepulchres, which indeed appear beautiful outward, but are within full of dead men's bones, and of all uncleanness. Even so ye also outwardly appear righteous unto men, but within ye are full of hypocrisy and iniquity."

Dark and terrible as is this picture, I hold it to be strictly true of the overwhelming mass of professed Christians in America. They strain at a gnat, and swallow a camel. Could any thing be more true of our churches? They would be shocked at the proposition of fellowshipping a *sheep*-stealer; and at the same time they hug to their communion a *man*-stealer, and brand me with being an infidel, if I find fault with them for it. They attend with Pharisaical strictness to the outward forms of religion, and at the same time neglect the weightier matters of the law, judgment, mercy, and faith. They are always ready to sacrifice, but seldom to show mercy. They are they who are represented as professing to love God whom they have not seen, whilst they hate their brother whom they have seen. They love the heathen on the other side of the globe. They can pray for him, pay money to have the Bible put into his hand, and missionaries to instruct him; while they despise and totally neglect the heathen at their own doors.

Such is, very briefly, my view of the religion of this land; and to avoid any misunderstanding, growing out of the use of general terms, I mean, by the religion of this land, that which is revealed in the words, deeds, and actions, of those bodies, north and south, calling themselves Christian churches, and yet in union with slaveholders. It is against religion, as presented by these bodies, that I have felt it my duty to testify.

I conclude these remarks by copying the following portrait of the religion of the south, (which is, by communion and fellowship, the religion of the north,) which I soberly affirm is "true to the life," and without caricature or the slightest exaggeration. It is said to have been drawn, several years before the present anti-slavery agitation began, by a northern Methodist preacher, who, while residing at the south, had an opportunity to see slaveholding morals, manners, and piety, with his own eyes. "Shall I not visit for these things? saith the Lord. Shall not my soul be avenged on such a nation as this?"

"A PARODY.

"Come, saints and sinners, hear me tell
How pious priests whip Jack and Nell,
And women buy and children sell,
And preach all sinners down to hell,
  And sing of heavenly union.

"They'll bleat and baa, dona like goats,
Gorge down black sheep, and strain at motes,
Array their backs in fine black coats,
Then seize their negroes by their throats,
  And choke, for heavenly union.

"They'll church you if you sip a dram,
And damn you if you steal a lamb;
Yet rob old Tony, Doll, and Sam,
Of human rights, and bread and ham;
    Kidnapper's heavenly union.

"They'll loudly talk of Christ's reward,
And bind his image with a cord,
And scold, and swing the lash abhorred,
And sell their brother in the Lord
    To handcuffed heavenly union.

"They'll read and sing a sacred song,
And make a prayer both loud and long,
And teach the right and do the wrong,
Hailing the brother, sister throng,
    With words of heavenly union.

"We wonder how such saints can sing,
Or praise the Lord upon the wing,
Who roar, and scold, and whip, and sting,
And to their slaves and mammon cling,
    In guilty conscience union.

"They'll raise tobacco, corn, and rye,
And drive, and thieve, and cheat, and lie,
And lay up treasures in the sky,
By making switch and cowskin fly,
    In hope of heavenly union.

"They'll crack old Tony on the skull,
And preach and roar like Bashan bull,

Or braying ass, of mischief full,
Then seize old Jacob by the wool,
  And pull for heavenly union.

"A roaring, ranting, sleek man-thief,
Who lived on mutton, veal, and beef,
Yet never would afford relief
To needy, sable sons of grief,
  Was big with heavenly union.

"'Love not the world,' the preacher said,
And winked his eye, and shook his head;
He seized on Tom, and Dick, and Ned,
Cut short their meat, and clothes, and bread,
  Yet still loved heavenly union.

"Another preacher whining spoke
Of One whose heart for sinners broke:
He tied old Nanny to an oak,
And drew the blood at every stroke,
  And prayed for heavenly union.

"Two others oped their iron jaws,
And waved their children-stealing paws;
There sat their children in gewgaws;
By stinting negroes' backs and maws,
  They kept up heavenly union.

"All good from Jack another takes,
And entertains their flirts and rakes,
Who dress as sleek as glossy snakes,

And cram their mouths with sweetened cakes;
And this goes down for union."

Sincerely and earnestly hoping that this little book may do something toward throwing light on the American slave system, and hastening the glad day of deliverance to the millions of my brethren in bonds—faithfully relying upon the power of truth, love, and justice, for success in my humble efforts—and solemnly pledging my self anew to the sacred cause,—I subscribe myself,

FREDERICK DOUGLASS.

LYNN, *Mass., April 28, 1845.*

THE END.

ENDNOTES

1. See the *Washington Post* Web site for the complete transcript of the speech: www.washingtonpost.com/wp-srv/politics/documents/ Obama_Hispanic_Chamber_Commerce.html
2. NBC television news coverage from 1969 of Angela Y. Davis's fight against the Gov. Ronald Reagan–led effort to have her fired can be seen on *YouTube* here: www.youtube.com/watch?v=AI4U-q2o2cg
3. In defiance of the regents, Davis began teaching prior to the Superior Court of Los Angeles issuing a decision in her favor on the grounds that firing for political beliefs is unconstitutional.
4. When Mumia Abu-Jamal calls collect from Death Row his personal conversations are always fifteen minutes in length. The conversations are repeatedly interrupted by recorded messages from the prison and at the fifteenth minute the state automatically disconnects the call.
5. Written exchange between Mumia Abu-Jamal and Greg Ruggiero dated February 25, 2009, and posted to *Z-net* at this address: www.zmag. org/znet/viewArticle/20677.
6. Transcript of a talk by Angela Y. Davis given on February 15, 2008, at Metropolitan State College, Denver. An audio recording of the talk is available from Alternative Radio, www.alternativeradio.org. Text of the talk will appear in the book by Angela Y. Davis, *The Meaning of Freedom*, forthcoming from City Lights Books.
7. Angela Y. Davis. *Women, Race & Class* (Random House: New York, 1981), p. 30.
8. Ibid. p. 51.
9. Davis grew up in a neighborhood of Birmingham, Alabama, called "Dynamite Hill," so named because of the frequency of bombings there by white terrorists against the neighborhood's black residents. She also personally knew Carol Robertson, Cynthia Wesley, and the

247

two other girls who were murdered by the 16th Street Baptist Church bombing, September 15, 1963.

10. Lincoln, who when meeting *Uncle Tom's Cabin* author Harriet Beecher Stowe in 1862 allegedly exclaimed, "So you are the little woman who wrote the book that started this great war!," believed that the primary directive of the North was to preserve the Union and *not* to end slavery. During the heat of the Civil War he wrote a letter to the *New York Tribune* saying, "If I could save the Union, without freeing the slaves, I would do it. If I could do it by freeing some and leaving others alone, I would do that. What I do about slavery and the coloured race, I do because I believe it would help to save the Union."

11. Angela Y. Davis and Eduardo Mendieta. *Abolition Democracy: Beyond Empire Prisons, and Torture* (Open Media Series/Seven Stories Press, 2005). Quotation is from the introduction by Eduardo Mendieta, page 12.

12. Original quoted from *The Life and Times of Frederick Douglass*: "My hands were no longer tied by my religion."

13. Angela Y. Davis and Eduardo Mendieta. *Abolition Democracy: Beyond Empire Prisons, and Torture* (Open Media Series/Seven Stories Press, 2005).

14. Philip Foner, ed. *The Life and Writings of Frederick Douglass, Vol. I*, New York: International Publishers, 1950, p. 59.

15. See Waldo E. Martin, Jr. *The Mind of Frederick Douglass*, Chapel Hill and London: University of North Carolina Press, 1984, pp. 22–25.

16. H. Bruce Franklin. *Prison Literature in America: The Victim as Criminal and Artist*, New York: Oxford University Press, 1989.

17 . Harriet Jacobs. *Incidents in the Life of a Slave Girl Written by Herself*, edited by Jean Fagan Yellin, Cambridge, Massachusetts: Harvard University Press, 1987, p. 201.

18. Frederick Douglass, Harriet Jacobs, *Narrative of the Life of Frederick Douglass, An American Slave*; Anthony Appiah, Introduction, New York: Modern Library, 2000. p. xv.

19. Ibid.

20. Ibid., p. 102

21. Ibid., pp. 103–104

22. Frederick Douglass. *Narrative of the Life of Frederick Douglass,* Introduction by Deborah McDowell, Oxford University Press, 1999, p. xx.

23. Here McDowell draws from Jenny Franchot, "The Punishment of Esther: Frederic Douglass and the Construction of the Feminine" in Eric J. Sundquist, ed., *Frederick Douglass : New Literary and Historical Essays.* Cambridge: Cambridge University Press, 1990.

24. McDowell, Intro, p. xxl.

25. Ibid., p. 61.

26. Ibid., p. 61.

27. McDowell, Intro., p. xxv.

28. Speech on West Indian Emancipation, August 3, 1857.

29. See Angela Y. Davis, *Women, Race, and Class,* New York: Random House, 1981, p. 9.

30. Original quoted from *The Life and Times of Frederick Douglass:* "O God, save me! God, deliver me! Let me be free! Is there any God? Why am I a slave?"

31. Original quoted from *The Life and Times of Frederick Douglass:* "That slave who had the courage to stand up for himself against the overseer, although he might have many hard stripes at first, became while legally a slave virtually a free man. 'You can shoot me,' said a slave to Rigby Hopkins, 'but you can't whip me', and the result was he was neither whipped nor shot."

32. From *The Life and Times of Frederick Douglass.*

33. Original quoted from *The Life and Times of Frederick Douglass:* "Personality swallowed up in the sordid idea of property! Manhood lost in chattelhood! . . . Our destiny was to be fixed for life, and we had no more voice in the decision of the question that the oxen and cows that stood chewing at the haymow."

34. Original quoted from *The Life and Times of Frederick Douglass:* "He had no choice, no goal, but was pegged down to one single spot, and must take root there or nowhere."

35. Original quoted from *The Life and Times of Frederick Douglass:* "His going out into the world was like a living man going out of sight and hearing of wife, children, and friends of kindred tie."

36. Original quoted from *The Life and Times of Frederick Douglass:* " 'If you

give a nigger an inch he will take an ell. Learning will spoil the best nigger in the world. If he learns to read the Bible it will forever unfit him to be a slave. He should know nothing but the will of his master, and learn to obey it.'"

37. Original quoted from *The Life and Times of Frederick Douglass*: "'Very well,' thought I. 'Knowledge unfits a child to be a slave.' I instinctively assented to the proposition, and from that moment I understood the direct pathway from slavery to freedom."

38. Original quoted from *The Life and Times of Frederick Douglass*: "When I was about thirteen years old, and had succeeded in learning in read, every increase of knowledge, especially anything respecting the free states, was an additional weight to the most intolerable burden of my thought—'I am a slave for life.' To my bondage I could see no end. It was a terrible reality, and I shall never be able to tell how sadly that thought chafed my young spirit."

39. Original quoted from *The Life and Times of Frederick Douglass*: "Liberty, as the inestimable birthright of every man, converted every object into an asserter of this right. I heard it in every sound, and saw it in every object. It was ever present to torment me with a sense of my wretchedness, the more horrible and desolate was my condition. I saw nothing. Without seeing it and I heard nothing without hearing it. I do not exaggerate when I say that it looked at me in every star, smiled in every calm, breathed in every wind and moved in every storm."

40. Original quoted from *The Life and Times of Frederick Douglass*: "She aimed to keep me ignorant, and I resolved to know, although knowledge only increase my misery."

41. Quoted from *The Life and Times of Frederick Douglass*.

42. Original lecture quoted from *The Life and Times of Frederick Douglass*: "If he has got religion, thought I, he will emancipate the slaves ... Appealing to my own religious experience, and judging my master by what was true in my own case, could not regard him as soundly converted, unless some such good results followed his profession of religion."

43. Original lecture quoted from *The Life and Times of Frederick Douglass*: "I will teach you, young man, that though I have parted with my sins, I

have not parted with my sense. I shall hold my slaves and go to heaven, too."

44. Original lecture quoted from *The Life and Times of Frederick Douglass*: "Captain Auld could pray, I would fain pray; but doubts arising, partly from the shame religion which everyone prevailed, there was awakened in my mind a distrust of all religion and the conviction that prayers were unavailing and delusive."

45. Original lecture quoted from *The Life and Times of Frederick Douglass*: "I was whipped, either with sticks or cowskins, every week. Aching bones and a sore back were my constant companions. Frequently as the lash was used, Mr. Covey thought less of it as a means of breaking down my spirit that that of hard and continued labor. He worked me steadily up to the point of my powers or endurance. From the dawn of day in the morning till the darkness was complete in the evening, I was kept hard at work in the fields or the woods."

46. Original quoted from the *The Life and Times of Frederick Douglass*: "His plan was never to approach in an open, manly and direct manner the spot where his hands were at work. No thief was ever more artful in his devices than this man Covey. He would creep and crawl in ditches and gullies, hide behind stumps and bushes, and practice so much of the cunning of the serpent, that Bill Smith and I, between ourselves, never called him by any other name than 'the snake.'"

47. Original quoted from the *The Life and Times of Frederick Douglass*: ". . . with Mr. Covey, trickery was natural. Everything in the shape of learning or religion which he possessed was made to conform to the semi-lying propensity. He did not seems conscious that the practice hand anything unmanly, bas or contemptible about it."

48. From *The Life and Times of Frederick Douglass.*

49. Quoted from *The Life and Times of Frederick Douglass.*

50. Original quoted from *The Life and Times of Frederick Douglass*: "I do not know; at any rate, I was resolved to fight, and what was better still, I actually was hard at it. The fighting madness had come upon me, and I found my strong fingers firmly attached to the throat of the tyrant, as heedless of consequences, at that very moment, as if we stood as equals before the law. The very color of the man was forgotten."

51. Original quoted from *The Life and Times of Frederick Douglass*: "He was frightened, and stood puffing, and blowing, seemingly unable to command words or blows."

52. Original quoted from *The Life and Times of Frederick Douglass*: "Now, you scoundrel, go to your work; I would not have whipped you half so hard if you had not resisted.' . . . The fact was, he had not whipped me at all. He had not, in all the scuffle, drawn a sing drop of blood from me. I had drawn blood

53. This is the same man who gave me the roots to prevent my being whipped by Mr. Covey. He was "a clever soul." We used frequently to talk about the fight with Covey, and as often as we did so, he would claim my success as the result of the roots which he gave me. This superstition is very common among the more ignorant slaves. A slave seldom dies but that his death is attributed to trickery.

54. She was free.

55. I had changed my name from Frederick Bailey to that of Johnson.

56. I am told that colored persons can now get employment at calking in New Bedford—a result of anti-slavery effort.

ABOUT THE AUTHORS

ANGELA Y. DAVIS

Angela Y. Davis is Professor Emerita of History of Consciousness at the University of California and author of eight books. She is a member of the executive board of the Women of Color Resource Center, a San Francisco Bay Area organization that emphasizes popular education of and about women who live in conditions of poverty. Having helped to popularize the notion of a "prison-industrial complex," she now urges her audiences to think seriously about the future possibility of a world without prisons and to help forge a twenty-first-century abolitionist movement. Her most recent books are *Abolition Democracy* and *Are Prisons Obsolete?*, both published in the Open Media Series.

FREDERICK DOUGLASS

The son of an enslaved black woman and an unknown white man, "Frederick Augustus Washington Bailey" was born into slavery around 1818 in Maryland. After a failed attempt to free himself in 1836, he succeeded in escaping on September 3, 1838. Once free, Frederick Douglass became a public speaker, editor, best-selling author, organizer for the anti-slavery movement, and statesmen. His first book, *Narrative of the Life of Frederick Douglass, an American Slave*, was published in 1845 and became an immediate best-seller. His second book, *My Bondage and My Freedom*, was published in 1855, and his final book, *Life and Times of Frederick Douglass*, was published after the Civil War, in 1881. Douglass gave public talks in the United States and abroad and became the leading black voice in the anti-enslavement movement. Douglass lived to become a trusted advisor to Abraham Lincoln, United States Marshal for the District of Columbia, Recorder of Deeds for Washington, D.C., and U.S. Minister-General to Haiti.

OPEN MEDIA SERIES

Open Media is a movement-oriented publishing project committed to the vision of "one world in which many worlds fit"—a world with social justice, democracy, and human rights for all people. Founded during wartime in 1991 by Greg Ruggiero, Open Media has a history of producing critically acclaimed and best-selling titles that address our most urgent political and social issues.

City Lights Books | www.citylights.com